Chicago Public Library

REFERENCE

Form 178 rev. 11-00

REFERENCE LIBRARY OF BLACK AMERICA

ELEMENTARY SCHOOL EDITION

Secretary of State Colin Powell. *Photograph by Scott Applewhite. Reproduced by permission of AP/Wide World Photos.*

REFERENCE LIBRARY OF BLACK AMERICA

ELEMENTARY SCHOOL EDITION

ALMANAC

VOLUME 3

CULTURE

JAY P. PEDERSON AND KENNETH ESTELL,

EDITORS

DISTRIBUTED EXCLUSIVELY BY AFRICAN AMERICAN PUBLICATIONS

Reference Library of Black America: Almanac
Elementary School Edition

Jay P. Pederson and Kenneth Estell, *Editors*

STAFF

Carol DeKane Nagel, *U•X•L Developmental Editor*
Thomas L. Romig, *U•X•L Publisher*

Amy Marcaccio, *Acquisitions Editor*

Barbara A. Wallace, *Permissions Associate (Pictures)*
Margaret A. Chamberlain, *Permissions Supervisor (Pictures)*

Mary Kelley, *Production Associate*
Evi Seoud, *Assistant Production Manager*
Mary Beth Trimper, *Production Director*

Mary Krzewinski, *Cover Design*
Cynthia Baldwin, *Art Director*

The Graphix Group, *Typesetter*

ISBN 0-7876-5898-7 (Set)
ISBN 0-7876-5899-5 (Volume 1)
ISBN 0-7876-5900-2 (Volume 2)
ISBN 0-7876-5901-0 (Volume 3)
ISBN 0-7876-5902-9 (Volume 4)
ISBN 0-7876-5903-7 (Volume 5)

Printed in the United States of America

Published by Gale Group Inc.

ABOUT AFRICAN AMERICAN PUBLICATIONS:

African American Publications is committed to providing students and adult researchers with accurate, authoritative, and accessible information on a wide variety of ethnic and ethno-religious groups in the United States and Canada. In addition to Americans of African heritage, African American Publications also offers a variety of reference sets covering Hispanics, Asian Americans, Native Americans, Middle Eastern Americans, Americans of European descent, and notable American men and women.

To find out more about these publications, kindly contact us at 215-321-7742 or via e-mail at afriampub@aol.com. Please visit us at our new online biographical site at www.africanpubs.com.

GUIDE TO THE REFERENCE LIBRARY:

Almanac: Features a comprehensive range of historical and current information on African American life and culture. Organized into 26 chapters, including Civil Rights, The Family and Health, and Science, Medicine, and Invention.

Chronology: Explores significant social, political, economic, cultural, and educational milestones in black history. Arranged by year and then by month and day, the chronology spans from 1942 to modern times.

CONTENTS

Volume 2: Society

Volume 3: Culture

PICTURE CREDITS

The photographs and illustrations appearing in *African American Almanac* were received from the following sources:

Courtesy of the Library of Congress: pp. 3 (upper left), 4, 7, 91, 97, 107, 181, 214, 215, 219, 220, 221, 224, 226, 233, 246, 258, 259, 270 (lower right), 273 (lower right), 283, 317, 319, 351, 353, 431, 534, 558; **AP/Wide World Photos:** pp. 10, 12, 14, 18, 19, 20, 51, 86, 94, 108, 113, 122, 140 (lower right), 144, 146, 153, 155, 157, 161, 171, 231, 235, 244, 254 (upper right), 260, 262 (upper left), 262 (upper right), 265, 269 (upper left), 270 (upper left), 275, 281, 286, 291 (lower right), 292, 293 (lower right), 312, 318, 324 (lower right), 326 (lower right), 328, 356, 359, 374, 377, 378, 382, 418, 419, 427, 428 (upper left), 434 (lower right), 437, 440 (upper left), 440 (lower right), 443, 444, 447, 450, 451, 457, 458, 460, 462, 463, 467, 470, 471, 482, 483, 484, 492, 495 (lower right), 497, 498, 499, 502, 503, 505, 508, 514, 516, 527, 538, 543 (upper right), 546 (upper left), 547, 548, 550 (lower right), 551 (upper left), 552, 553, 554, 555, 560, 576, 577, 578, 579; **UPI/Bettmann:** pp. 13, 28, 105, 112, 120, 230, 238, 254 (upper left), 256, 280, 288, 291 (upper left), 293 (upper left), 307, 428 (upper right), 452, 468, 469, 478, 506, 513, 525, 541, 544, 549, 551 (lower right); *Harper's Magazine:* pp. 22, 147; **United Nations:** pp. 27, 33, 36, 42, 44, 48, 59, 61, 63 (upper left), 63 (lower right), 65, 67, 71, 385; **National Museum of African Art:** pp. 31, 35, 39; **Courtesy of Fisk University:** pp. 77, 95, 247, 272, 354 (lower right), 371, 422 (lower right), 430; **Bettmann Archive:** pp. 89, 172, 229 (lower right), 357, 453, 504, 535 (lower right), 559; **Courtesy of the Consulate General of Jamaica:** p. 102; **NBC:** 110, 466, 500; **The Granger Collection, New York:** p. 138; **The Schomburg Center for Research in Black Culture, the New York Public Library:** pp. 158, 512, 545; **Courtesy of the National Park Service:** p. 166, 168; **U.S. Navy:** 174, 572; **Denver Public Library, Western Collection:** pp. 176, 180; **Archive Photos/Lass:** p. 223; **Archive Photos:** pp. 252, 271, 384, 454, 455, 456, 459, 465, 515, 543 (upper left); **Courtesy of the NAACP:** pp. 264, 285, 290, 311, 320 (lower right), 331; **Courtesy of the New York Public Library:** pp. 269 (lower right), 434 (upper left), 495 (upper left); **Surlock Photographers:** p. 274; **Courtesy the National Archives:** pp. 284, 303, 521; **Reproduced by**

permission of The Stanley B. Burns, M.D. Collection: pp. 299, 379; **NASA:** p. 306; **Photograph by Sue Stetler:** p. 309; **Photograph by Kenneth Estell:** pp. 310, 334, 336; **Photograph by Andy Roy:** pp. 314, 324 (upper left), 326 (upper left); **Courtesy of the Walker Collection of A'Lelia Bundles:** p. 320 (upper left); **Photograph by Brian V. Jones:** 330, 333, 341; **Courtesy of the Bethune Museum and Archive:** p. 354 (upper left); **Photograph by Bruce Giffin:** p. 362; **Photograph by Beverly Hardy:** p. 364; **The National Portrait Gallery, The Smithsonian Institution:** p. 370; **Archive Photos/American Stock Photos:** p. 373; **John Duprey/*NY Daily News:*** p. 381; **Springer/ Bettmann Film Archive:** pp. 423, 493; **Courtesy of the Arthur B. Spingarn Collection, Moorland-Spingarn Research Center, Howard University:** p. 424 (upper left); **Courtesy WABC-TV, New York:** p. 442; **Courtesy of The Associated Publishers:** p. 475; **Archive Photos/Frank Driggs Collection:** p. 494; **Courtesy of Columbia Records:** p. 496; **Courtesy of the William Morris Agency:** p. 509; **Courtesy of *Downbeat:*** p. 510; **National Museum of American Art, Washington D.C./Art Resource, N.Y.:** pp. 520 (upper left), 523, 531; **General Motors, Public Relations Department:** p. 526; **Reuters/Bettmann:** p. 546 (lower right); **Photograph by Carl Nesfield:** p. 550 (upper left); **U.S. War Department/National Archives:** p. 563, 564; **U.S. Army:** p. 567, 569, 573.

WORDS TO KNOW

A

abolition: the destruction or ending of slavery; an *abolitionist* is a person or a group in favor of putting an end to slavery, or the principles behind such a person or group

abstain: to refrain from doing; *abstinence* is the act of voluntary avoiding a certain behavior

acquittal: a court decision freeing one of charges; to be *acquitted* is to be cleared of all charges, to be declared not guilty

aesthetics: the study or theory of beauty as it relates to art

affiliates: those businesses or persons associated or connected with an organization

affirmative action: a policy designed to correct the effects of racial and sexual discrimination through hiring quotas and other measures; sometimes negatively referred to as "reverse discrimination"

agrarian: relating to farming, agriculture, or agribusiness

alliance: a close partnership or association

alma mater: (Latin for *fostering mother*) the particular school or college a person attended

alumni: persons who have attended or graduated from a particular school or college

American Dream: the concept that all Americans, given equal opportunities, may strive for personal and financial success

anchor: in broadcasting, to serve as chief reporter of a newscast

annex: to add or attach

anthropology: the study of humans, including their characteristics, culture, and customs

anti-Semitism: discrimination or prejudice against Jews

apartheid: a policy of racial separation

applied arts: fields in which art serves a dual function, such as graphic or fashion design

apprehension: an understanding of an issue; fear that something bad will occur; capture or arrest

appropriations: funds set aside for a specific purpose

arbiter: one who judges or decides

archaeologists: scientists who study past civilizations, especially by a process of careful digging called excavation

archipelago: a group of islands

archives: a place where important papers, documents, and other memorabilia are kept; the papers, documents, and memorabilia that are kept in such a place

arias: melodies in an opera, oratorio, or cantata created especially for a solo voice

Armageddon: the place referred to in the Biblical Book of Revelation where the last battle is to be fought between the forces of good and evil; the time of the last battle; also referred to as the *apocalypse*

aspirations: ambitions

assimilate: to become like or similar to, to join

attaché: a person with special duties, particularly in connection with international relations

autonomous: independent or self-governing

avant-garde: new and nontraditional

B

bequest: money or other personal property that is awarded by means of a will; the act of giving money or personal property

Black Muslim movement: also called the Nation of Islam; a religious movement, begun by W. D. Fard and furthered by Elijah Muhammad, that preached black self-sufficiency and worship of Allah. Among the most famous converts to the Black Muslims were Malcolm X and Muhammad Ali

Black codes: unfair rules and laws directed at African Americans following emancipation

Bohemianism: living outside the conventions of society

bourgeoisie: a social class between the wealthy and the working class; the middle class

boycott: a refusal by an individual or group to buy, sell, or use products or services

C

capital: money, property, and other valuable assets that are used to start and sustain a business

cardiovascular: the system that links the heart and blood vessels

catafalque: a wooden framework used to hold a coffin during elaborate funerals

catalysts: persons or objects that bring about events or results

caucus: a group of politicians or a meeting of political party leaders

ceded: formally transferred or surrendered

census: an official count of the population that also includes information about age, sex, race, economic status, etc.

CEO: *C*hief *E*xecutive *O*fficer; the highest executive of a company or organization

charter: a document that outlines the goals of a group

chattel: persons regarded as fixed items of personal property

choreography: the arrangement or step-by-step planning of a dance

civil disobedience: nonviolent resistance to a policy or law; first popularized by Indian leader Mohandas (Mahatma) Gandhi

clichés: unoriginal statements or ideas

coalition: a group united in purpose

collateral: a form of security that is offered to a lender until a loan is repaid

commercialism: business focused purely on profit

compromise: something blending qualities of two different things

compulsory: necessary or required

confrontations: bold face-to-face meetings

conglomerate: a large corporation that owns several smaller businesses in a number of different industries

connoisseurs: those who take keen enjoyment in their field of expertise

conscientious: ruled by what one thinks to be right

consecrated: made or *ordained* a bishop through a religious ceremony; made or declared sacred

consensus: general agreement

conservatism: a political movement or philosophy that stresses less government and more private enterprise

conspiracy: a plot to work together in secret, especially for harmful or unlawful purposes

constituency: the group of voters an elected official serves

constitutionality: legality in relationship to the laws and principles set forth in the Constitution

controversial: subject to argument or debate

conversion: the change from lack of faith to religious faith; the change from one religion to another

corporations: businesses, formed with permission of the state or federal government, that have the power to own property and make contracts

coup: (short for the French *coup d'état*) a quick seizure of power, often by military force

crossover: the ability to please or appeal to more than one group

curators: heads of museums or special collections

curriculum: the standard information, teaching plan, and testing for a course or major field of study; the entire teaching program of a given school or college

D

defected: left because of disagreement

demographics: the census characteristics of a population, broken down by geographic regions

denigrated: belittled

denomination: a specific religious body or organization (for example, Baptist, Methodist, or Catholic); *denominational* means having to do with a specific religious group, the opposite of *nondenominational*

deportation: the sending away, by official order, of an undesirable alien

deposed: removed from office

derive: come from

dialect: a spoken language specific to a region or group

diaspora: a scattering or dispersion of people who share a common background

dictatorships: governments ruled by absolute power; the opposite of democracies

dilemma: a serious problem, usually one for which there are two equally difficult choices

dioceses: a religious district presided over by a bishop; large or prominent religious districts are called *archdioceses*

disenfranchised: the poor or disadvantaged

dissenting: in legal matters, a *dissenting* opinion is one that differs from the majority, or ruling, opinion; dissenting opinions are offered by justices who think their fellow members on the bench have made an error in their ruling

documentary: a nonfiction (true-to-life) film

dominion: the power to rule; a territory that is ruled

downsizing: trimming, through plant closings, layoffs, etc., to make a business healthier and more profitable

E

ecumenical: anything promoting the unity of Christian churches

effigy (to burn in): to publicly burn an image of a person in protest

emancipation: to be freed from the control of another

enact: to pass into law

enclave: a territory or group that is surrounded by a larger territory or group

endowment: a gift, generally money, to an institution or person; a natural talent or ability

entrepreneurship: the business quality of undertaking risk for the sake of earning a profit

equatorial: near or of the equator, the imaginary line equidistant from the North and South Poles

equity: value or worth, as in money, property, stocks, etc.

eulogized: praised after death

Eurocentric: concerned primarily with European or Western culture

evangelists: literally, bringers of good news; those fervently devoted to spreading the gospel

execution: the act of legally putting to death; carrying out of a task

exile: a person who by force or choice lives outside his country; the condition of living outside a country

exodus: literally, a going out; a massive migration or departure of a people

exonerated: declared not guilty

exploitation: unfair use of an individual or group

F

fascism: government by a one-party dictatorship

fertility: the state of being able to produce children, determined by age and other factors

feudal: a system popular in Europe during the Middle Ages in which serfs were bound for

life to work the land and were, in turn, protected by overlords

fine arts: fields in which art stands alone, such as painting or sculpture

flamboyant: flashy and exciting

franchise: in sports, a team that is granted membership in a league

fugitive: a person who flees from danger or from the law

G

generative: capable of continuing, through reproduction, etc.

genocide: the destruction or killing of an entire race

genre: a type of literary form, such as a poem, story, novel, essay, or autobiography

glaucoma: an eye-related disorder that can, if untreated, cause a total loss of vision

Gothic: a style of architecture that stresses pointed arches and steep roofs; a style of fiction that suggests horror, mystery, and gloom; anything ornate

H

Harlem Renaissance: a flowering of black literature and performing arts during the 1920s in which Harlem served as the artistic capital

heptathlon: a track and field contest consisting of seven separate events

I

illiterate: a person who cannot read or write; the phrase *functional illiterate* refers to those whose reading and writing abilities are less than adequate

impeached: brought before a hearing on charges of wrongdoing

importation: to bring into a new region goods that are then usually sold

inauguration: the formal ceremony by which a person is placed in office; to be *inaugurated* is to be formally sworn into office

incumbent: the current office-holder

indemnity: protection

indentured servant: a person bound by contract to work for another for a certain length of time; during the early period of American history, both black and white indentured servants were commonly used and were usually forced to work for seven years before they gained their freedom

indigo: a plant of the pea family; the blue dye obtained from such a plant

inducted: enrolled or entered into

inevitably: predictably

infringement: the act of overstepping boundaries and intruding on another's

injunction: an order from the court either prohibiting or demanding a certain action

innovators: in the performing arts, those who introduce new methods and styles and thereby change the direction of the field

inoculation: an injection, aimed at disease prevention, that causes a mild form of the disease; the injection forces the body to build up an immunity to a later attack of the actual disease

institution: a person, thing, idea, or practice that has taken root or settled into habit

insurmountable: not able to be overcome

integration: the bringing together of races, classes, or ethnic groups that were previously separated; bringing a group into equal membership in society

interpretive: bringing out the meaning or importance of

intimidation: to scare or make timid by means of threats or violence

intravenous: directly into a vein

involuntary servitude: the institution of forcing people to work for their freedom; also called indentured servitude

ironically: in a manner opposite of what is expected

J

Jim Crow: a reference (taken from a minstrel song) to laws and practices supporting the segregation of blacks and whites

jurisdiction: legal territory

L

laypersons: nonordained church members; also referred to as the *laity*

leveraged buyout: the purchase of a company in which most of the sale price is financed using borrowed money

liable: responsible by law

liberal arts: a course of study that provides a broad background in literature, philosophy, languages, history, and abstract sciences; the opposite of a vocational or technical course of study

literacy: the ability to read and write

litigation: the process of filing and pursuing a lawsuit

liturgical: having to do with the order and nature of public worship, including the songs, rituals, readings, prayers, and sermon that form a religious service

lynching: murder without trial, frequently by hanging

M

maligned: spoken ill of

manumission: liberation from slavery; to be *manumitted* is to be freed from slavery

Maroons: black slaves who escaped and formed communities in the mountains, swamps, and forests of the southern colonies

Mason-Dixon line: generally thought of as the line that divides the North and the South; named after surveyors Charles Mason and Jeremiah Dixon, who in 1767 settled a dispute over the east-west boundary between Pennsylvania and Maryland and the north-south boundary between Maryland and Delaware

Masonic: having to do with Masons or Freemasons, an international organization dedicated to universal brotherhood, charity, and mutual aid

media: a plural noun signifying all types of communication (radio, television, newspapers, etc.)

median: the midway point in a series of numbers (half of the numbers being above and half below); not to be confused with average

metaphor: a figure of speech in which one thing is identified with another

Middle Passage: the trade route from West Africa across the Atlantic Ocean to the West Indies and the East Coast of America

militant: aggressive; prepared to fight

minstrel: an entertainer typically associated with a traveling comic variety show, such as the Christy Minstrels (from which the word comes)

misogyny: hatred of women

monarchy: a government ruled by a king or queen or other person of royal birthright. Constitutional monarchies are limited in power, but absolute monarchies are essentially dictatorships

monographs: scholarly books or articles on a single subject

Monroe Doctrine: the policy established by President James Monroe that said the United States would not allow European interference in the affairs of America or her neighbors

mosaics: pictures composed of small bits of stone, glass, tile, etc.

mulatto: a person who has one black and one white parent; any person of black-white ancestry

multicultural: concerned with minority as well as majority cultures

N

nationalism: a movement to achieve independence; patriotism; a *nationalist,* in black studies, is one who believes in the creation of black power through a politically and economically strong black nation

negritude: the awareness among blacks of their cultural heritage

neoclassical: art or literature dating from the mid-seventeenth to mid-eighteenth century that revived the classic forms and styles of ancient Greece and Rome

niche: a desirable place; in business terms, typically a safe market not threatened by competitors

O

odyssey: epic journey

ordained: established or invested with the title of minister, priest, rabbi, and so forth

orthodox: traditional; conforming to established doctrine

ostracized: banished

P

pacify: to satisfy or calm

Pan-Africanism: a theory or movement embracing cooperation and unity among African nations and among all African peoples

parodied: poked fun at through imitation

patents: legal and exclusive rights to produce, use, and sell what one has invented

pathology: the condition and results of a disease

patois: a differing form of a standard language

patron: a person, usually wealthy, who finances and supports another person, cause, or institution; *patronage* is that support given

pending: not yet decided or determined

per capita: per person

petition: a formal, signed request

philanthropists: those who share their wealth with various humanitarian, or charitable, causes

plaintiffs: those filing a lawsuit (*defendants* are those being accused or sued by the plaintiffs)

plasma: the fluid part of blood

plebiscite: an expression of the people's will, by ballot, on a political issue

posthumous: after death

poverty: the condition of being poor; the government determines poverty according to a poverty index based on monetary income alone; in 1990 a family of four was considered to be in poverty if the household income was less than $13,359

predecessors: those who have gone before, usually said of influential persons

prenatal: taking place before birth

proclamation: an official announcement

prohibit: to forbid or make illegal; something *prohibited* is not allowed by law

prolific: highly energetic and productive

propaganda: ideas and information used to further or to hinder a movement or cause

propagation: expansion from person to person, place to place; reproduction or multiplication

prosperity: wealth

protectorate: a weaker state that is governed by a stronger state

proteges: persons guided, taught, or shaped by generally older and more influential persons

provision: something set aside for the future; a section in a legal document that outlines a special condition or requirement

psychedelic: causing intense stimulation of the mind

pueblo: a close-knit village of sun-dried bricks and stone built by Native Americans in the southwestern United States; Pueblo Indian cultures include the Hopi and Zuni

pundits: experts or authorities on given topics

R

ratify: to approve or pass

ratio: the relationship of one quantity to another, expressed in a fraction or percentage

recession: a general decline in business activity that translates into more layoffs, fewer new jobs, and decreases in household spending power

referendum: a direct vote by the people

repatriationist: one who believes in returning to the country of origin

repeal: to cancel

repertoire: songs or pieces within a musician's or group of musicians' typical performance program

repertory: a group that alternates the works (from their *repertoire*) that they perform

repression: the act of keeping back, putting down, or holding down

resolutions: statements of intent

retaliation: to respond in kind, as in "an eye for an eye"

retrospective: an exhibit that looks back at an artist's development

rhetoric: especially effective speaking or writing; alternately, language that is flashy but insincere

rigorous: very strict or challenging

S

savanna: a grassland

schism: a split or break within an organization, usually as a result of serious disagreement

secession: withdrawal from an organization

secular: relating to worldly things, as opposed to religious or spiritual things

segregation: the separation or isolation of a race, class, or ethnic group into a restricted area

seminary: a school where one is trained to become a minister, priest, or rabbi

separatism: a policy of keeping the races apart in all matters

seriocomic: mixing serious and comic elements

servitude: slavery

sociologist: one who studies human society

sole proprietorships: businesses in which the owner is also the chief operator

sovereignty: having dominion status or control over a nation

speaking in tongues: a gift of the Holy Spirit described in the New Testament (see Acts 2:4 and 1 Corinthians 12-14)

stereotypes: simple and inaccurate images of a person, group, etc.

stigmatizes: marks or brands unfavorably

subservient: inferior or subject to rule by another

suppression: keeping from happening or being known

supremacy: the state of having the most power or authority; a *supremacist* is one who believes in the superiority of a certain group

surveillance: continual observation

syncopated: shifted in beat from what is regularly accented to what is regularly unaccented

syndicated: sold and presented through many *media* outlets

syphilis: a venereal, or sexually transmitted, disease that can lead to a weakening of the bones, nerve tissue, and heart

T

temperance: in general, the quality of self-restraint; historically, movements promoting moderation, total avoidance, or prohibition of alcoholic liquor

tenure: a permanent right to a position, as in teaching

thesis: in education, a long, formal research paper

timpanist: a player of kettledrums (timpani)

tumultuous: troubled or characterized by upheaval

U

ultimatum: a final offer that, if rejected, will leads to a specific consequence

unalienable: secure from being transferred or taken away

unanimously: in total agreement

uncompromising: unwilling to change one's principles or alter one's behavior

unconstitutional: not permitted or spelled out in the United States Constitution; one of the primary duties of the Supreme Court is to determine whether laws or customs are constitutional or unconstitutional

Underground Railroad: a secret network of safe places, such as houses or barns, where runaway slaves could hide on their way north; these safe places were called "stations," and the people who operated them were called "conductors"

V

v.: an abbreviation for versus, a term used to separate opposing forces, such as the plaintiff and the defendant in a lawsuit

valets: personal servants who take care of clothes, help one dress, etc.

vaudeville: a form of entertainment consisting of skits, dances, songs, and other performances

versatile: multitalented

viability: ability to grow and prosper

Victorian: a nineteenth-century style of architecture characterized by largeness and ornamentation; anything dating from the reign of Queen Victoria (1837-1901)

virtuoso: someone with extraordinary skill in a given field

vulnerable: open to attack or injury

W

West Indies: a large group of islands, including the Bahamas, Puerto Rico, Jamaica, Cuba, Haiti, and the Virgin Islands, that lies between North and South America and to the east of Central America

Western Hemisphere: that half of the world containing the continents of North and South America; also called the New World

women's suffrage: a movement for the right of women to vote

REFERENCE LIBRARY OF BLACK AMERICA

ELEMENTARY SCHOOL EDITION

18

Literature

African American Writers, Scholars, and Poets

FACT FOCUS

- Although Phillis Wheatley is often called America's first black author, Jupiter Hammon was almost certainly the first black American whose work appeared in print. Hammon published his first poem, "An Evening Thought: Salvation by Christ with Penitential Cries," in 1760.
- The earliest surviving slave account is Briton Hammon's *A Narrative of the Uncommon Suffering and Surprising Deliverance of Briton Hammon,* also published in 1760.
- By date of authorship, Lucy Terry was the first black American poet. In 1746 she wrote her only known poem, "Bars Fight," which was inspired by an Indian ambush of haymakers in the Bars, a small plateau near Deerfield, Massachusetts. The poem, however, was not published until 1855.
- William Wells Brown published the first travel book, *Three Years in Europe* (1852), the first novel *Clotel; or, The President's Daughter: A Narrative of Slave Life in the United States* (1853), and the first drama, *Experience; or How to Give a Northern Man a Backbone* (1856) by an African American.
- Charles W. Chesnutt, author of *The Conjure Woman* (1899), was the first major African American fiction writer.
- Poet Paul Laurence Dunbar was the first black writer to gain national fame and the first to support himself completely by his writing.
- Gwendolyn Brooks was the first black to win a Pulitzer Prize for poetry with *Annie Allen,* published in 1950. Brooks was also the first black woman admitted to the National Institute of Arts and Letters.

"I like clear simple images, clear simple **metaphors,** *making clear simple statements about not-so-clear, not-so-simple human beings."—Nikki Giovanni, in her* Racism 101 *(1994)*

"We die. That may be the meaning of life. But we do language. That may be the measure of our lives."—Toni Morrison, in her Nobel address before the Swedish Academy in Stockholm, December 7, 1993

Toni Morrison

Perhaps the single greatest moment in the history of African American literature was the Nobel Prize acceptance speech of writer Toni Morrison. Upon the announcement of the award in October 1993, black scholar Henry Louis Gates, Jr., said: "This is a great day for African-Americans, and for Americans in general. Just two centuries ago, the African-American literary tradition was born in slave narratives. Now our greatest writer has won the Nobel Prize."

Certainly there have been many other high points in the history of black literature: Maya Angelou's reading at the inauguration of President Bill Clinton in 1993; the awarding of Nobel Prizes to Nigerian Wole Soyinka in 1986 and West Indian Derek Walcott in 1992; the warm public reception given Richard Wright's *Native Son* in 1940. But none has so fully symbolized black writers' struggle for recognition.

When Morrison's novel *Beloved* was published in 1987, it was hailed as a masterpiece, particularly among fellow African American writers. However, when the book failed to win the 1987 National Book Award or the National Book Critics Circle Award, 48 well-known black writers and critics signed a tribute to Morrison's career and published it in the January 24, 1988, edition of the *New York Times Book Review*.

The document suggested that despite Morrison's growing international fame, her own country still owed her greater recognition. The recognition came, amid continuing

Zora Neale Hurston

called the only truly original American literary **genre.** However, another tradition was at work even before the spread of slavery in America. This was the oral tradition, in which African folktales were told and retold and adapted to fit new surroundings and circumstances.

None of these tales were collected into book form until Joel Chandler Harris published *Uncle Remus: His Songs and His Sayings* in 1880. Harris was a Georgia-born white writer who made his reputation by drawing upon the tales he had heard as a child. One of his first and most popular tales (which actually appeared in magazine form in 1879) was "Brer Rabbit, Brer Fox, and the Tar Baby" (see below for a discussion of Morrison's *Tar Baby*).

Harris unveiled a rich tradition of creation stories, moral tales, and comic narratives, and these were eventually researched and retold by twentieth-century black writers, most notably Zora Neale Hurston in *Mules and Men* (1935) and *Tell My Horse* (1938). Many of the tales have become classics and rank among the best examples of regional and **dialect** writing in American history.

controversy, when she won the 1988 Pulitzer Prize for fiction. Robert Christopher, the secretary of the Pulitzer board, stated: "[It] would be unfortunate if anyone diluted the value of Toni Morrison's achievement by suggesting that her prize rested on anything but merit." If there were any lingering doubts about Morrison's rank as a leading American, as well as leading global, writer, the 1993 Nobel Prize served to quell them. Morrison, finally, had achieved her rightful position in the literary world.

The Oral Tradition

The African American literary tradition was indeed born in slave narratives, as Gates said. In fact, slave narratives have been

Early African American Writers

Due to educational and racial barriers, only a handful of early African American writers made a name for themselves. Among these was Phillis Wheatley, who distinguished herself as a poet in the tradition of English writer Alexander Pope. Her first poem was printed in 1770 under the title "A Poem by Phillis, A Negro Girl on

A SURVEY OF TONI MORRISON'S NOVELS

The Bluest Eye (1969) centers around Pecola Breedlove, a black girl approaching adolescence, who desperately wants to be loved. Overwhelmed by the message—from movies, teachers, her own family—that the blonde-haired, blue-eyed, fair-skinned appearance of Shirley Temple is beautiful, she concludes that the reason she is teased and hated is that she is black and therefore ugly. Violated time and again by other characters, Pecola finally retreats into madness, believing that she is the most beloved little girl of all because she has the bluest eyes of all.

Morrison begins *The Bluest Eye* with: "Here is the house. It is green and white. It has a red door. It is very pretty." She repeats the passage twice. The second version resembles the first but is written without standard capitalization and punctuation. The third version is run together without spaces. Each version represents a type of family. The first version represents a white family; the second, a struggling yet happy black family; and the third, Pecola's family. Critics have praised this first novel by Morrison as an excellent study of black girlhood in America.

Sula (1973) explores the life and death of a black community called The Bottom in the town of Medallion, Ohio, by focusing on the friendship, which began in childhood, between two very different women, Sula Peace and Nel Wright. Nel grows up to marry, have children, and otherwise adapt to what society and her community expect of her. Sula, on the other hand, embarks on what the narrator calls an "experimental life," becoming an outcast by violating the codes of the community.

Because Morrison does not point to any single best interpretation of morality in this novel, she is able to touch virtually all readers. *Sula* was nominated for the 1975 National Book Award in fiction and also won the Ohioana Book Award that year.

Song of Solomon (1977) follows Milkman Dead as he sets out on a journey south from his Ohio home in hopes of recovering lost family treasure. What he finds is not gold, however, but the spiritual wealth of his rich family history.

Morrison casts the story in the pattern of myth and **odyssey** and draws upon an African American folktale about a group of African-born slaves who rise up from the plantation and fly back home across the ocean. *Song of Solomon* became a paperback best-seller and received the 1977 National Book Critics Circle Award and the 1978 American Academy and Institute of Arts and Letters Award.

Tar Baby (1981) takes place mainly on a tiny West Indian island named Isle des Chevaliers, after a group of mythical African horsemen. According to the legend, these blind horsemen—who were imported to work as slaves but were never actually enslaved—are still riding the hills.

Against this backdrop, Morrison stages a modern adaptation of the African American folktale of Tar Baby and Brer Rabbit, in which a farmer devises a tar baby as a lure to trap the rabbit, who has been raiding gardens.

Continued on next page

A SURVEY OF TONI MORRISON'S NOVELS

Once captured, Brer Rabbit outwits the farmer by begging not to be thrown into the briar patch, which is of course his only real haven. In Morrison's novel, the character of Jadine parallels that of Tar Baby. She falls in love with a handsome outlaw named Son, but finds that she cannot adapt to his ways, nor he to hers.

Several critics objected to the complex plot of *Tar Baby,* but most acknowledged it as an ambitious work, which overcomes its flaws thanks to the eloquence of Morrison's voice and the richness of her language. *Tar Baby* made the *New York Times* best-seller list and also helped earn Morrison a cover story in *Newsweek.*

Beloved (1987) is a masterfully told ghost story and study of family and community that focuses on the theme of slavery and its harmful legacy. The story begins with Sethe, who lives with her daughter Denver on the outskirts of Cincinnati in a farmhouse haunted by the ghost of Sethe's murdered baby daughter.

Paul D., a fellow slave of the Kentucky plantation from which Sethe escaped, comes to live with them. He violently casts out the baby spirit, or so they believe, until one day a beautiful young stranger arrives, calling herself "Beloved." Taking control of the household, Beloved feeds on Sethe's memories and explanations, nearly destroying her mother. Finally, the community of former slave women who have **ostracized** Sethe and Denver after

the murder join together to drive Beloved away.

In 1988 *Beloved* won both the Pulitzer Prize for fiction and the Robert F. Kennedy Award. The novel was also a finalist for the 1987 National Book Critics Circle Award and the 1987 National Book Award. Inspired by the true-life story of a runaway slave, *Beloved* is considered Morrison's finest work of fiction.

Jazz (1992) is Morrison's most experimental novel and is mainly set in Harlem during the Jazz Age of the 1920s. One of the novel's primary themes is the power that the city—with its music, freedom, optimism, and excitement—exerts over its black citizens. The results are often harmful and sometimes openly violent. For example, a married, middle-aged salesman named Joe Trace has an affair with an 18-year-old named Dorcas. After the affair has ended, he kills her. Trace's wife, Violet, then adds to the tragedy with a striking display of vengeance at Dorcas's funeral.

Like Morrison's earlier fiction, *Jazz* contains several complex characters, in addition to those mentioned, who are journeying toward self-discovery. Although their pasts are frequently marred by both private and collective miseries, there is always the chance for renewal and rebirth. One of the novel's primary messages is delivered by Violet's friend Alice, who says, "You got anything left to you to love, anything at all, do it."

the Death of Reverend George Whitefield." Unfortunately, like many other black writers of the time, Wheatley chose existing forms and topics of literary expression, and thus

her insights into African American culture were minimal.

Jupiter Hammon, George Moses Horton, and Frances Harper were poets who did

Phillis Wheatley

work (which many at the time believed could not have been written by a former slave), the *Narrative* also ranks with some of the best of all American autobiographies.

As the bonds of slavery were loosened, black writers clamored to be heard, but the range of their work was generally limited. Gradually, though, it began to broaden, especially during the 1890s in the work of Paul Laurence Dunbar. Before his untimely death in 1906, Dunbar had become the dominant presence in the world of American Negro poetry. Yet despite his accomplishments, Dunbar found himself trapped in the undesirable role of a dialect poet, for his poems and stories—written on current themes and in standard English—were unpopular with white readers.

manage to address the evils of slavery and racism in their works. Yet, because they followed styles ill-suited to their subject matter, their verse seems stiff and unnatural to later critics. As a whole, such early black writers are today less appreciated for their literary talents than for the social and historical value of their writings.

By the mid-nineteenth century, however, exceptions to the rule began to appear. No doubt the most notable was Frederick Douglass. Although known mainly as a brilliant abolitionist speaker, journalist, and statesman, Douglass is also recognized as the author of the most popular slave account in American history, the *Narrative of the Life of Frederick Douglass, an American Slave, Written by Himself,* published in 1845. An extraordinary

Paul Laurence Dunbar, whom Booker T. Washington called the "Poet Laureate of the Negro Race"

Langston Hughes

White society still remained the chief **arbiter** of literary taste. This was because much of publishing in America was white-controlled and the work of blacks was often filtered and distorted through this lens. As a result, literature by African Americans attempted to prove that blacks could fit into middle-class American society. In fact, much of the African American literature of this era aimed to create the image that blacks were happy with their lot in life. Dunbar, Chesnutt, and others did try to break the chains of this imposed expression and attempted to present black life as it really was, not as society wanted it to be. But their efforts were largely unappreciated.

Although the accomplishments of writers of this era were remarkable, existing conditions prevented African American writers from truly flourishing. Above all, these writers paved the way for the Harlem Renaissance and prompted authors to think about and develop a truly African American culture.

The Harlem Renaissance

The Harlem Renaissance spanned the era from the middle of World War I through the early 1930s. Scholars have suggested several starting dates for the movement, including the publication of Claude McKay's poems "The Harlem Dancer" (1917) and "If We Must Die" (1919), as well as Langston Hughes's "The Negro Speaks of Rivers" (1921). Whatever the case, the Renaissance gained force as African American artists and writers from around the country entered and reacted to the thriving artistic community of Harlem. At the same time, another hub of artistic activity was taking place in Washington, D.C. In fact, Harlem artists often traveled to Washington for a break and a new perspective.

The conscious agenda of these mostly young artists was to define and celebrate black art and culture and to change the false notions most Americans had of black life. As *Crisis, Opportunity,* and other African American journals began to appear, it became much easier for black writers to publish in a style that suited their tastes. Also, African American writers were finding that some white **patrons** in the publishing fields were, in fact, interested in promoting their work. **Bohemianism** was flourishing, and many of the Harlem Renaissance artists fit this label. Called "New Negroes,"

1925 poster announcing the first literary contest sponsored by the African American journal *Opportunity*

addition to these figures, the Renaissance writers owed a huge literary debt to Jessie Fauset and Alain Locke. As literary editor of *Crisis,* Fauset discovered and published early works by Hughes, McKay, and Jean Toomer, among others. And Locke became both the spokesperson and authority of the movement with his anthology *The New Negro,* published in 1925.

The Harlem Renaissance was marked by a shift away from moralizing work, which was characteristic of earlier writing that decried racism. Even though much of this writing was eloquent, Du Bois, Locke, and others realized that it was doing very little to change the consciousness of the country.

Alain Locke

they sought to chisel out a unique, African-centered culture for blacks and to improve race relations while maintaining a distinct cultural identity.

Important writers of this era included Hughes, McKay, Countee Cullen, Nella Larsen, and Hurston. These younger writers were aided by the older, established writers, critics, and editors, including W. E. B. Du Bois, with his journal, *Crisis,* and Charles S. Johnson, editor of *Opportunity,* which sponsored many literary contests. In

For this reason, they decided instead to challenge these new writers to produce works that came directly out of personal experience—to communicate the ills of the racist world with art rather than essay. In this way, readers were not struck so bluntly with the grim realities presented by African American writers. Writers were able to deliver more subtle, and perhaps more effective, messages by portraying the lives of characters and by composing verse.

African American Writers after the Harlem Renaissance

As the economic depression deepened, the Harlem Renaissance slowly faded. The publication of Richard Wright's *Native Son* in 1940 marked a new era in the life of African American literature. The years from 1940 to 1955 served as a transition period for black letters. They bridged the wildly creative period of the Renaissance with the more intense creativity and political activity that was to define the work produced during the civil rights movement.

With the publication of his classic novel, Wright maintained that the era of the Harlem Renaissance—with its motto of "art for art's sake"—must die and be replaced instead with works directly intended to end racism.

During this time, other black writers, notably poets, were taking a different road. Gwendolyn Brooks, Melvin B. Tolson, and Robert Hayden used classical and mythical themes in their works, blending them with references to modern African American issues. This approach seemed to work, for their writing was accepted in the university community and beyond.

Dust jacket for Arna Bontemps's anthology covering the Harlem Renaissance. Bontemps was one of the most productive black writers of the twentieth century

Ralph Ellison's publication of *Invisible Man* (1952), arguably one of the best American novels of the twentieth century, and James Baldwin's *Go Tell It on the Mountain* (1953), were two other books that brought serious African American issues to mainstream culture. In addition, many African American works were gaining acceptance in the literary establishment and were being taught in English classes around the country.

The Black Arts Movement

The Black Arts Movement, or the Black Aesthetic Movement, has been the first

Ralph Ellison

ers of the Arts Movement consciously set out to define what it meant to be a black writer in a white culture.

For the most part, the black writers of this era were supportive of separatism and black nationalism. Rebelling against the mainstream society by being essentially anti-white, anti-American, and anti-middle class, these artists moved from the Renaissance view of art for art's sake into a philosophy of art for politics' sake.

The Black Arts Movement attempted to produce works of art that would be meaningful to the black masses. Towards this end, popular black music of the day, including John Coltrane's jazz and James Brown's rhythm and blues, as well as street talk, were some of the inspirational forces for their art. In fact, much of the language used in these works was vulgar and shocking—this was often a conscious attempt to show the vitality and power of black activists. These writers tended to be revolutionaries rather than diplomats—the movement favored Malcolm X over Martin Luther King, Jr. In addition, those who believed in the Black Arts Movement believed that black artists shared responsibility as political activists in the pursuit of nationalist goals.

Leading writers in this movement included Imamu Amiri Baraka (LeRoi Jones), whose poetry was as well known as his political abilities; and Haki R. Madhubuti (Don L. Lee), a poet and essayist who was overwhelmingly popular—selling over 100,000 copies of his books without a national distributor.

Ishmael Reed, on the other hand, an early organizer of the Black Arts Movement, later objected to some of the movement's doc-

major African American artistic movement since the Harlem Renaissance. Beginning in the early 1960s and lasting through the mid-1970s, this movement was not brought on by white patrons—as the Renaissance had been in part—but was fueled by the anger and activism of Wright, Ellison, and other notable African American writers of the mid-century.

This artistic movement closely paralleled the social and politically oriented civil rights and black power movements. While such phrases as "Black is beautiful" were being popularized, African American writ-

James Baldwin

trines. He became inspired more and more by the black magic and spiritual practices of the West Indies, in what he called the "Hoo-Doo Aesthetic." Sonia Sanchez, another leading voice of the movement, managed to combine feminism with her commitment to nurturing children and men in the fight for black nationalism.

Post-1960s Literature and the Rise of Black Women Writers

Many women, however, were writing in response to the Black Arts Movement, protesting the role they felt the male-oriented black nationalist movement had allotted them. They reclaimed Zora Neale Hurston's work and looked to it for inspiration. These women were also supported by the women's liberation movement, which allowed their works to reach a wider audience. In this way, the somewhat antifemale politics of the Black Arts Movement provoked women writers to express their own unique voice. Maya Angelou, Toni Morrison, Nikki Giovanni, Alice Walker, Gayl Jones, Jamaica Kincaid, Terry McMillan, and Gloria Naylor are examples of successful women authors who have become prominent figures in the publishing world. In fact, during the 1980s, African American women writers led publishing in both quality and quantity of work.

Because of the Black Arts Movement, African American writing and African American culture became more accepted in

Alice Walker

ing coups of the post-1950s era. With his novel, as well as the highly popular television miniseries that followed, many blacks became interested in their African ancestors and many non-blacks arrived at a deeper understanding of the African American experience.

Modern black writers seem to have shifted in tone from the literature of the 1960s. No longer is there as much emphasis on the contrasts between black and white in America. The themes of self-reflection and healing are evident in the words of Morrison, John Edgar Wideman, and Kristin Hunter; the works of these artists portray African Americans who do not allow the outer world to define them, who look to their own inner worlds for answers.

America in the 1970s and 1980s. This was especially true at the university level, for black studies departments emerged at campuses around the country. Variety was the key to contemporary African American writing, and barriers in various genres disappeared. For example, Octavia Butler and Samuel Delany broke into the world of science fiction and Donald Goines wrote detective fiction. The public welcomed novels of both folk history and the urban experience, and many artists, such as Alice Walker and Gayl Jones, found success writing in several genres.

Alex Haley's *Roots* (1976) was perhaps one of the greatest African American writ-

Alex Haley

19

Performing Arts

The African American in the Performing Arts

FACT FOCUS

- Henry Brown's *The Drama of King Shotaway* (1823) was the first play written and produced by an African American and performed on an American stage.
- *Trip to Coontown* (1898) was the first musical produced, written, and performed by African Americans on Broadway. Because of its clean break from **minstrel** entertainment, it ushered in a new era for blacks on the American stage.
- *Mulatto,* which opened in 1935, had the longest Broadway run of any nonmusical play written by an African American in the history of the American theater.
- Since its founding in 1958, the Alvin Ailey American Dance Theater has performed before more people throughout the world than any other American dance company.
- *The Wiz,* a Tony Award-winning play of 1975, became the longest-running black musical in the history of Broadway, with 1,672 performances.

"I don't care if you could stand on your eyebrows, if you was colored you couldn't get no work at all outside the black theater and night club circuits."—Moms Mabley, in the New York Post, *July 31, 1974*

"Freedom is a hard-bought thing."—Paul Robeson, in Here I Stand *(1958)*

African Americans and the Performing Arts

Since the earliest days of slavery, blacks have participated in and helped shape American performing arts. Of course, for the majority of this time they have done so in the face of prejudice, bigotry, and even cruelty. In the book *Black Magic,* Langston Hughes and Milton Meltzer document that "the first stage for the captive Africans was the open deck of a slave ship. There, on the way to the Americas, blacks in chains, when herded up on deck for exercise, were forced to sing and dance in the open air for the amusement of the crew."

Thomas "Blind Tom" Greene Bethune

After reaching the Southern plantations, Africans blended their native traditions, rhythms, and dances with a developing folk tradition, which together formed the basis for black American entertainment.

As singers, dancers, comedians, and bones players, slaves were often called upon to perform for their masters and, if talented enough, were even hired out to entertain others. Best remembered of the slave entertainers is Thomas "Blind Tom" Bethune, a talented pianist whose many concerts in the United States and Europe won fame for the pianist and profit for his owner, Colonel Bethune. (Blind Tom's story has been dramatized by Theodore Ward in the musical *Charity.*)

The Earliest Plays with African American Actors

The first performances by African American actors on the American stage were in plays authored by white playwrights who portrayed blacks as clowns or slow-witted characters. In 1769, for example, Lewis Hallam's comedy *The Padlock* was staged with a West Indian slave character named Mongo, who was a clown to be played by a black. Other white-authored plays from the period that depicted blacks in belittling roles were *Robinson Crusoe, Harlequin* (1792), and *The Triumph of Love* (1795), which included the native black character named Sambo.

The African Grove Theatre

New York City's free African American community founded the first black theater, the African Grove Theatre, in 1821. A group of amateur African American actors organized by Henry Brown, the Grove actors presented William Shakespeare's *Richard III* at the theater on October 1, 1821. The African Grove Theatre later produced Shakespeare's *Othello* and *Hamlet* and such lighter works as *Tom and Jerry* and *The Poor Soldier, Obi.*

One of the principal actors at the African Grove Theatre was James Hewlet, a West Indian-born black who distinguished himself in roles of *Othello* and *Richard III.* Hewlet later toured England and billed himself as "The New York and London Colored Comedian." Ira Aldridge, who relocated overseas and became one of the great Shakespearean tragic actors of the English stage, was also a member of the permanent group that performed at the African Grove Theatre. Aldridge was cast in comic and singing roles as well as in Shakespearean tragedies.

It was at the African Grove Theatre that the first play written and produced by an African American was performed on the

Poster advertising a minstrel performance

American stage. The play, presented in June 1823, was Henry Brown's *The Drama of King Shotaway.*

Because of disturbances created by whites in the audience, the local police raided the African Grove Theatre on several occasions. The theater evidently was wrecked by police and hoodlums during one of these raids, which forced its closing in late 1823. The group of black actors attached to the African Grove Theatre, determined to preserve their company, continued for several years to present plays at different rented locations throughout New York City.

Minstrel Shows

During the late 1820s and early 1830s white entertainers, observing the artistry of black performers, began to imitate blacks in their routines. Blackening their faces with burnt cork, these white entertainers performed jigs, jokes, and songs that poked fun at blacks.

White minstrel troupes in blackface became very popular on the American stage in the 1830s. Among some of the more famous white minstrel performers were Thomas Dartmouth Rice ("Daddy Rice"), the original "Jim Crow," Edwin Forrest and Dan Emmett, and the Christy Minstrels.

Some traveling white minstrel troupes used African American performers to enhance the realism of their productions. One such troupe was the Ethiopian Minstrels, whose star performer was William Henry Lane, an African American dancer who used the stage name "Master Juba" (inspired by an African dance called the juba). Lane was one of the greatest dancers of his generation. Throughout the United States and England, "Master Juba" was enthusiastically praised by audiences and critics alike. "Juba exceeded anything ever witnessed in Europe," one English critic, quoted by dance historian Marian Hannah Winter, wrote. "The manner in which he beats time with feet, and the extraordinary command he possesses over them, can only be believed by those who have been present at the exhibition" ("Juba and American Minstrelsy," *Chronicles of the American Dance,* edited by Paul Magriel, 1948).

Black minstrel troupes began to appear in the 1850s. But it was not until after the Civil War that they became established on the American stage. Although black minstrels inherited the negative **stereotypes** of blacks that white minstrels had established, the

African American performer won a permanent place on the American stage, providing a training ground for the many black dancers, comedians, singers, and composers to come.

Notable among these stage personalities were dancer-comedians Billy Kersands, Bert Williams, Bob Height, Dewey "Pigmeat" Martin, and Ernest Hogan; singers Gertrude "Ma" Rainey and Bessie Smith; and composers James Bland and William Christopher Handy. To a great extent, black minstrelsy created a national appreciation for the talent of black stage entertainers, drawing audiences to black shows and other forms of black entertainment for generations to come.

Reclaiming the Black Image: 1890 to 1920

By the 1890s black producers, writers, and stage performers sought to reform the demeaning images of blacks common to the American stage. *The Creole Show,* cast by black producer Sam Jack in 1891, was the first all-black musical to depart from minstrelsy. *The Creole Show* premiered in Boston in 1891 and later played at the Chicago World's Fair for the entire season. In 1895 black producer John W. Ishaw presented *The Octoroon,* another all-black musical that moved away from minstrel tradition. *Oriental America,* which Ishaw also produced, broke further from minstrel conventions by closing with an operatic medley.

Trip to Coontown, written and directed by Bob Cole in 1898, completely broke away from the minstrel tradition. The plot of this all-black musical was presented completely through music and dance. The first musical produced, written, and performed

Bert Williams and George Walker

by African Americans on Broadway, it ushered in a new era for blacks on the American stage.

Between 1898 and 1911, 13 all-black musicals opened on Broadway, showcasing the talents of black musicians, lyricists, directors, producers, and writers.

The highly popular *Clorinda: The Origin of the Cakewalk,* with music by composer Will Marion Cook and lyrics by poet Paul Laurence Dunbar, opened in 1898 at the Casino Roof Garden and featured comedian-singer Ernest Hogan. The comic-dance duo of Bert Williams and George Walker premiered their first Broadway musical, *The Policy Players,* in 1899. This success was followed by Williams and Walker's *Sons of Ham,* which played on Broadway for two seasons beginning in September 1900. Their *In Dohomey* premiered on Broadway in 1903 and, after a long run, toured successfully in England. *The Southerners,* with music by Will Marion Cook, opened on Broadway in 1904 with an interracial cast starring Abbie Mitchell. The Williams and Walker team returned to Broadway in 1906 with a new musical, *Abyssinia,* which consistently played to a full house.

In the same year the **versatile** Ernest Hogan appeared on Broadway in *Rufus Rastus.* In 1902 Hogan had starred in *Oyster Man,* which enjoyed a successful run on Broadway. Bob Cole, J. Rosamond Johnson, and James Weldon Johnson wrote and performed in *The Shoo-Fly Regiment,* another musical that opened on Broadway in 1902. Williams and Walker appeared in their last Broadway production together, *Bandanna Land,* in 1908. Bert Williams went on to appear in *Mr. Lord of Koal* on Broadway in 1909, and later was the star comedian performer in the *Ziegfield Follies.* The last black musical to open on Broadway before the 1920s was *His Honor the Barber* in 1911, with S. H. Dudley in the lead.

Black actors on the dramatic stage, like the performers in all-black musicals, were attempting to shed the lowly image of the African American projected by most white-produced minstrelsy and drama. The presentation of three plays—*The Rider of Dreams, Granny Maumee,* and *Simon the Cyrenian,* all by white playwright Ridgely Torrence—at the Garden Theatre in Madison Square Garden on April 5, 1917, was an exceptional and highly successful effort to portray blacks accurately on the dramatic stage.

Florence Mills

The Development of Black Performers from the Harlem Renaissance through the 1950s

Black Musicals

On May 23, 1921, *Shuffle Along* opened on Broadway, signaling the return of black musicals to the Great White Way and the arrival of the **Harlem Renaissance** on the American stage. Featuring the talented singer-dancer Florence Mills, *Shuffle Along* was written by Noble Sissle, Eubie Blake, Flournoy Miller, and Aubrey Lyles.

Mills quickly became a sought-after performer, appearing in *The Plantation Revue* (1922) before touring England. In 1926 Mills returned to Harlem and played the lead in *Black Birds* at the Alhambra Theatre.

Sissle and Blake returned to Broadway on September 24, 1924, with their new musical *Chocolate Dandies.* Two years later, Flournoy Miller and Aubrey Lyles opened on Broadway in *Runnin' Wild,* which introduced the Charleston to the country. Bill "Bojangles" Robinson, starring in *Blackbirds of 1928,* dazzled Broadway audiences with his exciting tap dancing style. And several other notable black musicals opened on Broadway during the 1920s, including *Rang Tang* (1927), *Keep Shuffling* (1928), and *Hot Chocolates* (1929).

Porgy and Bess opened on Broadway in 1935 and became the major all-black musical production of the decade. With music by George Gershwin, this folk opera became an instant success. Todd Duncan played Porgy and Ann Brown played Bess. Comedian-

Josephine Baker, the talk of Paris during the 1920s and 1930s

Paul Robeson as the Emperor Jones

dancer John Bubbles assumed the role of Sportin' Life.

In the 1940s black musicals were scarce on Broadway. *Cabin in the Sky,* starring Ethel Waters, Dooley Wilson, Todd Duncan, Rex Ingram, J. Rosamond Johnson, and Katherine Dunham and her dancers ran for 165 performances after it opened on October 25, 1940. *Carmen Jones,* perhaps the most successful all-black musical of the decade, opened in 1943 with Luther Saxon, Napoleon Reed, Carlotta Franzel, and Cozy Cove; it had a run of 231 performances and was taken on tour. In 1946 *St. Louis Woman,* featuring Rex Ingram, Pearl Bailey, Juanita Hall, and June Hawkins, played a short run to mixed reviews.

The Dramatic Theater

During the Harlem Renaissance years, the black dramatic actor remained less active than the black performer in musicals. White playwrights tended to create flawed portraits of African Americans in productions of serious dramas. This was true of Eugene O'Neill's lead character—a black American named Brutus Jones—in the *Emperor Jones.* A powerful character, Jones declares himself emperor of a West Indies island and is eventually defeated as much by his own fears and madness as by the natives he has brutally ruled. Recounting Charles Gilpin's performance as Jones at the Provincetown Theatre in 1920, critic Loften Mitchell noted that:

> This play, while offering one of the most magnificent roles for a Negro in the American theatre, is the first in a long line to deal with the Negro on this level. O'Neill obviously saw in the Negro rich subject matter, but he was either incapable or unwilling to deal directly with the matter. (*Black Drama, the Story of the American Negro in the Theatre,* 1967)

Nonetheless, African American actors and actresses had to accept the roles in which they were cast by white playwrights. In 1924 the O'Neill play *All God's Chillun' Got Wings* opened at the Provincetown Theatre starring Paul Robeson and Mary Blair. Because of its interracial theme, the play received mixed reviews.

Rose McClendon starred in Paul Green's Pulitzer Prize-winning *In Abraham's Bosom* in 1926, and was ably supported by Abbie Mitchell and Jules Bledsoe. Marc Connelly's *Green Pastures* opened on Broadway on February 26, 1930; with Richard B. Harrison playing "De Lawd," it ran for 557 performances and was taken on an extensive road tour.

Three plays by Langston Hughes that did treat the African American objectively were produced successfully on Broadway in the 1930s. *Mulatto,* which opened in 1935 and starred Rose McClendon and Morris McKenney, had the longest Broadway run of any nonmusical play written by an African American in the history of the American theater, with 373 consecutive performances. It was followed by *Little Ham* (1935) and *Troubled Island* (1936).

The Federal Theater Project

In the mid-1930s the Works Progress Administration (WPA) sponsored one of the greatest organized efforts to assist and encourage American actors, especially African American actors. The Federal Theater Project employed a total of 851 black actors to work in 16 segregated units of the project in Chicago, New York, and other cities from 1935 until 1939, when Congress ended the project. While the project was in operation, black actors appeared in 75 plays, including classics, vaudeville, comedy, and children's shows. Notable among the black actors who worked in the project and later became stars on Broadway and in film are Butterfly McQueen, Canada Lee, Rex Ingram, Katherine Dunham, Edna Thomas, Thomas Anderson, and Arthur Dooley Wilson.

The American Negro Theater

In the wake of the Federal Theater Project, the American Negro Theater was established in Harlem by Abram Hill, Austin Briggs-Hall, Frederick O'Neal, and Hattie King-Reeves. Its objective was to portray black life honestly and to give black actors and playwrights a forum for their talents. Some of their productions eventually made it to Broadway. In 1944 the theater produced Philip Yordan's *Anna Lucasta* in the basement of the 135th Street Library in Harlem. It was successful enough to move to Broadway, and featured Hilda Simms, Frederick O'Neal, Alice Childress, Alvin Childress, Earl Hyman, and Herbert Henry. Abram Hill's *Walk Hard* opened in Harlem in 1946, and later became a Broadway production with Maxwell Glanville in the lead. The American Negro Theater provided a training ground for many black actors who later became stars on Broadway and in Hollywood, including Ruby Dee, Ossie Davis, Harry Belafonte, and Sidney Poitier.

Dramatic Theater in the 1950s

The rise of television in the 1950s generally had a negative affect on the American theater. Employment for all actors fell sharply, especially for black actors. Ethel Waters did, however, open on Broadway in 1950 as the lead in Carson McCullers's *Member of the Wedding,* which was well-received. Louis Peterson's *Take a Giant Step* opened on Broadway in September 1953 to critical praise; in the cast were Frederick O'Neal, Helen Martin, Maxwell Glanville, Pauline Myers, Estelle Evans, and Louis Gossett, Jr.

One of the most successful all-black plays to appear on Broadway opened in March 1959. This was Lorraine Hansberry's

Raisin in the Sun, the first Broadway play written by a black woman and the first by any black to win the New York Drama Critics Award. Its cast included Sidney Poitier, Ruby Dee, Diana Sands, Claudia McNeil, Louis Gossett, Jr., Ivan Dixon, Lonnie Elder III, and Douglas Turner Ward.

Black Dance

Many performers in the early black musicals that appeared on Broadway from 1898 and 1910, such as George Walker and Bert Williams, were expert show dancers. Similarly, in the all-black musicals of the 1920s performers like Florence Mills and Bill "Bojangles" Robinson captivated audiences with their show dancing.

By the early 1930s black pioneers of modern dance were appearing on the dance stage. Four of these black **innovators** were Hemsley Winfield, Austin Asadata Dafore Horton, Katherine Dunham, and Pearl Primus.

Winfield presented what was billed as "The First Negro Concert in America" in Manhattan's Chanin Building on April 31, 1931. Two suites on African themes were performed, along with solos by Edna Guy and Winfield himself. In 1933 Winfield became the first black to dance for the Metropolitan Opera, performing the role of the Witch Doctor in *Emperor Jones.*

Daforc Horton, a native of Sierra Leone, electrified audiences in New York with his 1934 production of *Kykunkor.* Dance historian Lynne Fauley Emery concludes that *Kykunkor* "was the first performance by black dancers on the concert stage which was entirely successful. It revealed the potential of ethnic material to black dancers, and here-

Katherine Dunham in 1992

in lay Dafore's value as a great influence on black concert dance" (*Black Dance from 1619 to Today,* 2nd rev. ed., 1988).

Dunham had her first lead dance role in Ruth Page's West Indian ballet *La Guiablesse* in 1933. In 1936 Dunham received a master's degree in **anthropology** from the University of Chicago; her **thesis** was on *"The Dances of Haiti,"* the result of her on-site study of native dances in the West Indies. For the next 30 years, Dunham and her dance company toured the United States and Europe, dazzling audiences with her **choreography.** During the 1963-64 season, Dunham choreographed the Metropolitan Opera's production of *Aida,* becoming the first black American to do so.

Primus, like Dunham, was trained in anthropology. Her research in primitive

African dance inspired the first piece she performed as a professional dancer, *African Ceremonial,* presented on February 14, 1943. On October 4, 1944, in her Broadway debut at the Belasco Theater in New York, Primus performed dances of West Indian, African, and African American origin. The concert was widely acclaimed and launched her career as a dancer. Primus has traveled to Africa many times to research African dances. In 1959 she was named director of Liberia's Performing Arts Center. She later opened the Primus-Borde School of Primal Dance with her husband, dancer Percival Borde, and is currently involved in the Pearl Primus Dance Language Institute in New Rochelle, New York.

By the late 1950s several black dancers and dance companies were distinguishing themselves on the concert stage. Janet Collins was the "premiere danseuse" of the Metropolitan Opera Ballet from 1951 until 1954. Arthur Mitchell made his debut as a principal dancer with the New York City Ballet in 1955. Alvin Ailey established his company in 1958, and Geoffrey Holder, who made his Broadway debut in 1954 in *House of Flowers,* became a leading choreographer.

The Black Comedian

The earliest black comedians in America, like other early black entertainers, were slaves who in their free time entertained themselves and their masters. In the early minstrel shows, white comedians in blackface mocked blacks, to whom they referred as "coons." When African Americans began appearing in minstrel shows shortly after the Civil War, they found themselves burdened with the "coon" caricatures created by white performers. The dance-comedy team of Bert Williams and George Walker were the most famous of the early black comedians, appearing in numerous all-black musicals between 1899 and 1909.

A new comic movement emerged in the all-black musicals of the 1920s. This was the comedy of style, which emphasized such antics as rolling the eyes or shaking the hips. The venom and bite of black folk humor was replaced by a comedy of style that was more acceptable to the white audiences of these all-black musicals.

Real black folk humor, however, managed to survive and thrive in black nightclubs and black theaters such as the Apollo in Harlem and the Regal in Chicago in the 1930s, 1940s, and 1950s. In these settings, known as the "Chitterling Circuit," such black comedians as Tim Moore, Dusty Fletcher, Butterbeans and Susie, Stepin Fetchit, Jackie "Moms" Mabley, Redd Foxx, and Slappy White performed without restrictions.

The Civil Rights Movement and Its Affect on Black Performers

As the black civil rights movement challenged the national conscience in the 1960s, every facet of life of black Americans changed, including black performing arts. More plays about blacks by both black and white playwrights were produced, providing increased employment for black actors. On the dance stage there were more opportunities for blacks as composers, choreographers, and dancers. And many black comedians, by invitation, moved from the "Chitterling Circuit" to posh white nightclubs and theaters.

The Dramatic Theater

Three events in the 1960s signaled trends that would affect African American dramatic actors for the next 30 years: 1) the production of Jean Genet's play *The Blacks*; 2) the staging of LeRoi Jones's play *The Dutchman*; and 3) the founding of the Negro Ensemble Company.

The Blacks

On May 4, 1961, *The Blacks,* by French playwright/author Jean Genet, opened off-Broadway at the St. Mark's Theater. A play about African Americans written for white audiences, *The Blacks* provided employment for a host of black actors, including Roscoe Lee Browne, James Earl Jones, Louis Gossett, Jr., Helen Martin, Cicely Tyson, Godfrey Cambridge, Raymond St. Jacques, Maya Angelou, Charles Gordone, and many others.

Subsequently, black dramatic actors appeared on and off Broadway in several major plays by white playwrights. Notable among them were *In White America* by Judith Rutherford Marechal (1968), with Gloria Foster and Moses Gunn; *The Great White Hope* by William Sackler (1968), starring James Earl Jones; and *So Nice, They Named It Twice* by Neil Harris (1975), featuring Bill Jay and Veronica Redd.

The Dutchman

On May 23, 1961, the *Dutchman* opened at the Cherry Lane Theatre. In this revolutionary play, black actors were able to perform in roles that not only affirmed blackness, but portrayed the black power movement. Several black revolutionary plays followed, providing black actors with opportu-

nities. These included James Baldwin's *Blues for Mr. Charlie* (1964), with Al Freeman, Jr., and Diana Sands; and *The Toilet/The Slave* (1964) by LeRoi Jones (Imamu Amiri Baraka), starring James Spruill, Walter Jones, Nan Martin, and Al Freeman, Jr. In 1991 such black revolutionary plays as *General Hag's Skeezag* continued to provide important roles for black actors.

The Negro Ensemble Company

Perhaps most beneficial to black actors was the founding of the Negro Ensemble Company in New York in 1967. This theatrical production company, initially financed by a three-year grant of $1.2 million from the Ford Foundation, was the brainchild of playwright/actor Douglas Turner Ward. Housed first at the St. Mark's Theater and currently at Theater Four, the Negro Ensemble is headed by actor Robert Hooks as executive director, Gerald Krone as administrative director, and Ward as artistic director. The Negro Ensemble's goal is to develop African American managers, playwrights, actors, and technicians.

The Negro Ensemble has staged more than 100 productions, including the work of 40 black playwrights, and provided work for countless aspiring and veteran black actors. Several plays produced by the Negro Ensemble have eventually gone to Broadway, including Ward's *The River Niger* (1973), which won a Tony Award and an Obie Award, and Charles Fuller's Pulitzer Prize-winning *The Soldier's Play* (1981). A wealth of outstanding black actors and actresses have appeared in Ensemble productions, including Marshall Williams, Denise Nichols, Esther Rolle, Roxie Roker,

Sammy Davis, Jr.

Modern Black Musicals

The years from 1961 to the mid-1980s represented one of the most active periods for African American performers in musical theater. Many of the black musicals produced during these years, both on and off Broadway, enjoyed long runs and extended road tours.

Langston Hughes's musical *Black Nativity* opened on Broadway on December 11, 1961. Directed by Vinette Carroll, the cast was headed by gospel singers Marion Williams and the Stars of Faith, and also featured Alex Bradford, Clive Thompson, Cleo Quitman, and Carl Ford. Although it ran for only 57 performances on Broadway,

Ossie Davis (right) with co-star and wife (second from left), Ruby Dee, *Purlie Victorious,* 1961

Adolph Ceasar, Denzel Washington, Moses Gunn, and Barbara Montgomery.

Several black playwrights have had plays successfully produced on Broadway independent of the Negro Ensemble Company. Ntozake Shange's widely acclaimed *For Colored Girls Who Have Considered Suicide/When the Rainbow Is Enuf* (1972) had a cast of seven black women actresses. August Wilson's *Fences,* which opened on March 26, 1987, and featured James Earl Jones, won the 1987 Pulitzer Prize in drama. Wilson's *Two Trains Running,* which opened April 13, 1992, and starred Roscoe Lee Browne and Laurence Fishburne, received the New York Drama Critic's Award for 1992.

it went on to tour extensively throughout the United States and abroad.

In 1964 Sammy Davis, Jr., dazzled Broadway in Clifford Odets's *Golden Boy.* Davis was supported by a brilliant cast that included Robert Guillaume, Louis Gossett, Jr., Lola Falana, and Billy Daniels. *Golden Boy* ran for 586 performances.

Leslie Uggams and Robert Hooks appeared in *Hallelujah Baby,* which opened in New York's Martin Beck Theater on April 26, 1967. *Hallelujah Baby,* a musical look at five decades of black history, received a Tony Award and ran for 293 performances.

Purlie, based on Ossie Davis's 1961 play *Purlie Victorious,* opened on May 9, 1970, with Melba Moore and Robert Guillaume in lead roles. *Purlie* received good reviews and enjoyed a run of 688 performances.

Micki Grant's *Don't Bother Me, I Can't Cope,* starring Micki Grant and Alex Bradford, opened on April 19, 1972, to rave reviews. For this musical, which ran for 1,065 performances, Grant received a Drama Desk Award and an Obie award.

Virginia Capers, Joe Morton, and Helen Martin opened *Raisin,* based on Lorraine Hansberry's play *Raisin in the Sun,* on October 13, 1973. *Raisin* received the Tony Award for the best musical in 1974 and had a run of 847 performances.

Despite initially poor reviews, *The Wiz,* a black musical version of *The Wizard of Oz,* became a highly successful show. Opening on Broadway on January 5, 1975, *The Wiz* featured an array of talented performers, including Stephanie Mills, Hinton Battle, Ted Ross, Andre DeShields, Dee Dee Bridgewater, and Mabel King. *The Wiz* swept the Tony Award ceremonies in 1975 and became the longest-running black musical in the history of Broadway, with 1,672 performances.

Ain't Misbehavin', another popular black musical of the 1970s, opened on May 8, 1978. Based on a parade of songs composed by Thomas "Fats" Waller, *Ain't Misbehavin'* starred Nell Carter, Andre DeShields, Armelia McQueen, Ken Page, and Charlene Woodard. It played to Broadway audiences for 1,604 performances and Nell Carter received a Tony Award as best featured actress.

Two spectacular black musicals premiered on Broadway in the 1980s. *Dream Girls,* which opened at the Imperial Theater on December 20, 1981, captivated Broadway audiences with a cast that included Jennifer Holiday, Cleavant Derricks, Loretta Devine, and Cheryl Alexander. *Dream Girls* ran for 1,522 performances on Broadway and had an extensive road tour. For her role as Effie Melody White, Jennifer Holiday won a Tony Award. On April 27, 1986, Debbie Allen opened in the lead role of *Sweet Charity.* Reviews were favorable and the musical enjoyed a run of 386 performances, establishing Debbie Allen as a musical theater actress.

A few new all-black musicals have opened in the early 1990s, including *Five Guys Named Moe,* a tribute to musician Louis Jordan with Clarke Peters and Charles Augin, and *Jelly's Last Jam,* featuring Gregory Hines.

Modern Black Dance

Since the early 1960s two of the leading dance companies in the United States have

Alvin Ailey

been headed by black males and composed largely of black dancers. They are the Alvin Ailey American Dance Theater and the Dance Theater of Harlem.

The Alvin Ailey American Dance Theater

The Alvin Ailey American Dance Theater (actually founded in 1958) has performed before more people throughout the world than any other American dance company. With a touring circuit that has included 48 states and 45 countries, the Alvin Ailey American Dance Theater has been seen by more than 15 million people.

Today, the Alvin Ailey organization consists of three branches: the Alvin Ailey American Dance Theater, the Alvin Ailey

Repertory Ensemble, and the Alvin Ailey American Dance Center.

Between 1958 and 1988 the Alvin Ailey Dance Theater performed 150 works by 45 choreographers, most of whom were black. Notable among these black choreographers have been Tally Beatty, Donald McKayle, Louis Johnson, Eleo Romare, Billy Wilson, George Faison, Pearl Primus, Judith Jamison, Katherine Dunham, Ulysses Dove, Milton Myers, Kelvin Rotardier, and Gary DeLoatch. More than 250 dancers, again mostly black, have performed with the dance theater. Among its star performers have been Judith Jamison, Clive Thompson, Dudley Wilson, Donna Wood, Gary DeLoatch, George Faison, and Sara Yaraborough.

A **prolific** choreographer, Ailey created numerous works for his dance theater and other dance companies, including *Revelations* (1958); *Reflections in D,* with music by Duke Ellington (1962); *Quintet* (1968); *Cry* (1971); *Memoria* (1974); and *Three Black Kings* (1976). Ailey choreographed *Carmen* for the Metropolitan Opera in 1973 and *Precipice* for the Paris Opera in 1983.

The Alvin Ailey Repertory Ensemble (AARE) was established in 1974 as a training and performing company. Many of its graduates advance to the dance theater or perform with other dance companies. In 1988 the AARE had more than 100 members.

The Alvin Ailey American Dance Center is the official school of the Ailey organization. It attracts students from around the United States and abroad and offers a certificate in dance. The center's offerings include training in ballet, the Dunham Technique, jazz, and modern dance.

Moms Mabley with Merv Griffin, 1969

The Dance Theater of Harlem

In 1969 Arthur Mitchell, who established himself as one of the leading ballet dancers in the United States, and Karel Shook, a white ballet teacher, founded the Dance Theater of Harlem. The Dance Theater made its formal debut in 1971 at the Guggenheim Museum in New York City. Three of Mitchell's works premiered at this concert: *Rhythmetron, Tones,* and *Fête Noire.*

Today, the dance theater's **repertory** is wide-ranging. Among the most spectacular works performed by the theater are *Firebird, Giselle, Scheherazade,* and *Swan Lake.*

Some of the dancers who have had long associations with the theater are Lowell Smith, Virginia Johnson, Shelia Rohan, and Troy Game. Many of the theater's graduates have gone on to perform with other dance companies in the United States and Europe. The Dance Theater's school currently has about 1,000 students.

Notable Black Dancers

Between 1960 and 1990 several other black dancers have led distinguished careers in concert dance and show dancing. Among them have been Eleo Pomare, Debbie Allen,

443

Eddie Murphy's footprint is cast in cement, 1987

Ben Vereen, Rod Rogers, Fred Benjamin, Pepsi Bethel, Eleanor Hampton, Charles Moore, Garth Fagan, Carmen de Lavallade, and Mary Hinkson. Foremost among black choreographers have been Geoffrey Holder, Louis Johnson, and Donald McKayle. Some of the more prominent black dancers who are reviving the tap dance tradition are Chuck Green, Buster Brown, Honi Coles, Hinton Battle, Maurice and Gregory Hines, Lavaughn Robinson, and Nita Feldman.

Modern Black Comedy

Black comedians enjoyed greater exposure during the 1960s than ever before. No longer confined to the "Chitterling Circuit," such comedians as Jackie "Moms" Mabley, Redd Foxx, and Slappy White began to perform to audiences in exclusive white clubs as well as to audiences within the black community. They used black folk humor to comment on politics, civil rights, work, sex, and a variety of other subjects. Moms Mabley made two popular recordings: *Moms Mabley at the UN* and *Moms Mabley at the Geneva Conference.* In January 1972 Redd Foxx premiered on television as Fred Sanford in *Sanford and Son,* which remains one of television's most popular syndicated shows.

Several younger black comedians also became popular in the early 1960s. Dick Gregory used black folk humor to make political commentary. Bill Cosby specialized in amusing stories about boyhood in America. Godfrey Cambridge, although successful, did not rely on black folk humor. During the late 1960s and the early 1970s, Flip Wilson, who **parodied** historical and social experience by creating black characters who lived in a black world, became extremely popular on television. His cast of characters, which included "Freddy the Playboy," "Sammy the White House Janitor," and "Geraldine," were essentially black folk humor employed as social commentary.

Another vital black comedian who began his career in the 1960s was Richard Pryor. His well-timed and daring humor quickly won him a large group of faithful fans. Pryor, who has recorded extensively, has starred successfully in several films, including *Lady Sings the Blues, Car Wash,* and *Stir Crazy.*

During the 1980s and 1990s numerous black comedians have become successful in the various entertainment media. Eddie

Murphy made his first appearance on the television comedy series *Saturday Night Live* on November 15, 1980. From television, Murphy went on to Hollywood, making his movie debut in the film *48 Hours* in 1982. Starring roles followed in such films as *Beverly Hills Cop,* which was the highest-grossing comedy film in history, and *Coming to America.* Murphy has established his own company, Eddie Murphy Productions, to create and produce television and film projects.

Arsenio Hall came to prominence in 1987 as a successful guest host on the *The Late Show,* which won him a high-paying movie contract with Paramount Pictures. In 1988 Hall was featured with Eddie Murphy in the film *Coming to America,* and in January 1989 he debuted as host of his own highly successful late-night talk show. In mid 1994 Hall decided to pull out of the highly competitive late-night TV race and pursue other interests.

20

Film and Television

The African American
in Film and Television

FACT FOCUS

- Around 1912 William Foster produced the first short black film, *The Railroad Porter*.
- In 1914 the third film version of Harriet Beecher Stowe's *Uncle Tom's Cabin* was produced. This was the first full-length Hollywood film to feature a black actor (Sam Lucas) rather than a white actor in black-face.
- In 1919 Oscar Micheaux produced and directed *The Homesteader*, the first full-length black film. Micheaux also produced the first black sound film, *The Exile*, in 1931.
- The first black to receive an Oscar was Hattie McDaniel, who was honored as best supporting actress in the 1939 film *Gone with the Wind*.
- In 1965 Sidney Poitier became the first black to receive an Academy Award for best actor, for *Lilies of the Field*.
- The voice of Darth Vader in *Star Wars* (1977) and *The Empire Strikes Back* (1980), two of the highest-grossing films of all time, and *Return of the Jedi* (1983), was that of James Earl Jones, a highly respected black television, film, and stage actor.
- In 1992 John Singleton became the first African American to be nominated for best director by the Academy of Motion Picture Arts and Sciences. This same year Julie Dash became the first black woman writer and director to have a feature-length film open nationwide.

"I used to go to pictures and when I saw a Negro on the screen I always left the theater feeling embarrassment and uneasiness. There was the Negro, devoid of any dignity—good maids who laughed too loudly, good butlers afraid of ghosts. I want to make motion pictures about the dignity, nobility, the magnificence of human life."—Sidney Poitier

Spike Lee

"You gotta have the vision first. You gotta have it, you gotta go through school daze, you gotta do the right thing, and maybe, if you're lucky, you'll get mo' better. But you have to have that vision first."—Spike Lee, in By Any Means Necessary: The Trials and Tribulations of the Making of Malcolm X *(1992)*

FILM

In future histories of filmmaking, 1986 might well be cited as the most important turning point in history for black actors, directors, and producers. This was the year that Spike Lee released his first major picture, *She's Gotta Have It*. A comedy about a young woman's love life and three men who

> ## WORDS TO KNOW
>
> **clichés:** unoriginal statements or ideas
>
> **coalition:** a group bonded together by purpose
>
> **commercialism:** business focused purely on profit
>
> **crossover:** the ability to please or appeal to more than one group
>
> **documentary:** a nonfiction (true-to-life) film
>
> **exploitation:** unfair use of an individual or group
>
> **inducted:** enrolled or entered into
>
> **parodied:** poked fun at through imitation
>
> **seriocomic:** mixing serious and comic elements
>
> **stereotypes:** simple and inaccurate images of a person, group, etc.
>
> **uncompromising:** unwilling to change one's principles or alter one's behavior

compete for her affections, Lee's film was an instant hit with both critics and the public. Although made on a shoestring budget of $175,000, the film grossed over $7,000,000. Lee had proven that an African American filmmaker could make an artistically and financially successful black film that had universal appeal. Further, Lee had proven that all this—however difficult—could be done without the aid of Hollywood.

Close on the heels of Lee's movie came Robert Townsend's *Hollywood Shuffle*. Townsend's film, though released in 1987,

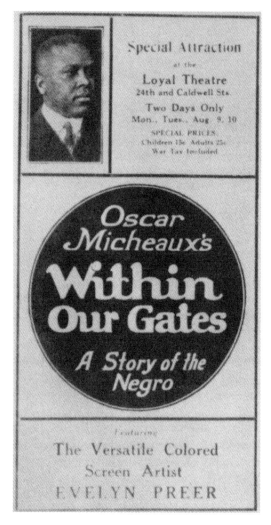

A poster from Oscar Micheaux's 1919 film *Within Our Gates*

Most importantly, though, both *She's Gotta Have It* and *Hollywood Shuffle* signalled an explosion in modern black filmmaking, which Hollywood has now come to recognize and support more earnestly than in the past. African Americans represent such a sizable part of the moviegoing public that Hollywood executives can ill afford to ignore their interests; in addition, Lee and Townsend have shown that there is a huge **crossover** potential for black-themed and black-directed movies. Among the most important new directors to follow in their path are John Singleton (*Boyz N the Hood*), Julie Dash (*Daughters in the Dust*), Mario Van Peebles (*New Jack City*), Bill Duke (*A Rage in Harlem*), and Matty Rich (*Straight out of Brooklyn*).

The Silent Era

During the early years of American filmmaking, it was a rarity for blacks to appear on screen, unless in low-budget, independently produced films. When a Hollywood film called for a black role, a white actor was typically chosen and then made up in burnt cork, or "blackface." When blacks did appear in Hollywood films, they, too, were generally forced to appear in blackface and were almost always limited to such unflattering roles as fool, servant, or slave. No matter the role, the black was nearly always shown as a dull-witted, superstitious coward.

The most famous film of this era was D.W. Griffith's 1915 epic *The Birth of a Nation,* which was inspired by Thomas Dixon's anti-black novel *The Clansman.* In the film, the Ku Klux Klan and the pre-Civil War South were glorified at the expense of blacks, who were portrayed as villains. A storm of controversy and protest surrounded

was actually begun some two and a half years earlier. It came in at the incredibly low cost of $100,000 but eventually earned more than $10,000,000. *Hollywood Shuffle* differed from the more straightforward *She's Gotta Have It* in that through a series of skits it **parodied** the white Hollywood establishment that forces black actors to perform according to a white view of reality.

the film's release and ultimately led to an increase in far more realistic, black-oriented films from outside Hollywood.

Oscar Micheaux and Early Independent Black Filmmaking

By the 1920s at least 30 independent black film companies were producing pictures for some 700 black movie theaters across the country. Yet even independently produced black films often followed Hollywood **stereotypes** of character and situation. For the most part these films were poorly produced and acted and made little effort to alter the already distorted black film image.

The most outstanding exceptions were the films of Oscar Micheaux. In 1918 the Lincoln Picture Co., an independent black film company, tried to buy the movie rights to *The Homesteader,* a novel Micheaux had published the previous year. When Micheaux insisted that he direct the planned movie, the deal fell through. Micheaux then went to New York, where he formed the Oscar Micheaux Corp. and completed the film. Between 1919 and 1948 Micheaux made 34 movies, including *Within Our Gates* (1919), which some film historians believe to be Micheaux's response to Griffith's *Birth of a Nation; Body and Soul* (1924), in which Paul Robeson made his first cinematic appearance; and *The Exile* (1931), the first black sound film.

While none of Micheaux's under-financed and hastily shot films won critical praise, they were popular with African American audiences and also attracted a limited white following. More importantly, the characters in Micheaux's films broke with the black stereotypes of the day: by and large, Micheaux's characters were middle- and upper-class blacks far removed from the servant life or the ghetto. Many black groups criticized Micheaux for this one-sided portrayal of black Americans. And one Micheaux film in particular, *God's Step Children* (1938), sparked public outcry for its portrayal of a light-skinned mulatto woman who wished to deny her black heritage.

Yet despite all his limitations as a filmmaker, Micheaux is still considered an important pioneer. The Black Filmmakers Hall of Fame has for two decades honored his name with its annual Oscar Micheaux Awards Ceremony, he was awarded a star on the Hollywood Walk of Fame, and he was **inducted** into the Directors Guild.

Blacks and Hollywood in the 1920s

After World War I the motion picture industry grew rapidly. More and more Americans sought movies as their chief form of entertainment and more and more blacks began to replace blackfaced whites on the screen. But, far from indicating any change in outlook, the newer Hollywood films employed blacks much the same as before—as vehicles for inciting cheap laughs from the audience.

Probably the most true-to-life depictions of blacks in this period were in Hal Roach's *Our Gang* comedies, in which black and white children played together naturally and generally as equals. Stars of these classic films include black child actors Allen Clayton (Farina) Hoskins, Matthew (Stymie) Beard, and William Henry (Buckwheat) Thomas.

However, there was little attempt to tap the acting potential of serious black actors. In 1928 black Americans took heart when

Bill "Bojangles" Robinson performing with Shirley Temple in the movie *The Little Colonel,* 1935

Paul Sloane of Fox was assigned to direct *Hearts in Dixie,* the first all-black, feature-length movie. But with its premiere in 1929 the film brought fresh disappointment, for it employed the same movie **clichés** regarding blacks. The only difference was that this production was on a grander scale than previous ones. Later that year, King Vidor of Metro-Goldwyn-Mayer (MGM) released *Hallelujah,* a more polished film that used several black actors, including Daniel Haynes and Nina Mae McKinney. However, these films still lacked real thoughtfulness about black American life.

The 1930s and the Dawn of Musicals

The good news was that the beginning of

sound in motion pictures—which came in 1927 with *The Jazz Singer*—meant a heightened demand in Hollywood, above all, for black musicians. Routines similar to those seen at the well-known Cotton Club in Harlem served as interludes for many dramatic pictures of this era. Yet **exploitation** was at the core of this trend. Although talented singers, dancers, and jazz musicians—including Lena Horne, Cab Calloway, and Louis Armstrong—appeared in countless all-black and mainstream Hollywood musicals, they were always segregated; films of this era never showed integrated jazz groups. And when films featuring blacks were distributed to Southern theaters, black musical sequences were often cut before the films were allowed to be shown to white audiences.

A notable exception to the sharp separation of blacks and whites on screen during the 1930s was the affectionate relationship between child actress Shirley Temple and veteran performer Bill "Bojangles" Robinson. During their dance routines, the pair lit up the screen in such films as *The Little Colonel* (1935) and *The Littlest Rebel* (1935).

Stepin Fetchit

Unfortunately, Hollywood's favorite black star during the decade, Stepin Fetchit, was one whose roles reinforced the myth of black inferiority. There were similar black stars of the era, notably Mantan Moreland and Willie "Sleep 'n Eat" Best, but none was as successful or as widely featured as Fetchit. In fact, Fetchit was the first black to receive major billing in American films. He was in such demand that within the span of ten years he is believed to have made at least

Stepin Fetchit

$2 million, a huge sum for any actor of the day, black or white.

Of course, Fetchit's place in movie history is a controversial one. While praised as an actor who opened the doors of Hollywood to other African Americans, he has also been criticized for bowing to racist stereotypes and doing little to raise the status of black actors. His characters—lazy, slow-witted, and subject to whites—have become so uncomfortable to watch that his scenes are sometimes cut when films in which he appeared are shown on television. Even at the height of his career, civil rights groups protested his roles, which they considered demeaning caricatures. Among Fetchit's films are *Hearts in Dixie* (1929), *Swing High* (1930), *Stand Up and Cheer* (1934), *David*

Harum (1934), *One More Spring* (1936), and *Zenobia* (1939).

Failed Attempts to Change Hollywood

One performer who tried to change Hollywood's conception of blacks was Paul Robeson, a talented stage actor and singer who also starred in such American films as *The Emperor Jones* (1933) and *Show Boat* (1936). However, Robeson had little success and he consequently made most of his films in England.

"Always Robeson went into a motion picture with the hope that it would elevate the state of his people," film scholar Donald Bogle wrote in his *Toms, Coons, Mulattoes, Mammies, & Bucks* (1989). "But after completing a role Robeson would discover that if anything his talents had been exploited and used to demean the black man's struggle for equality and full independence." This was true even of his foreign films.

Similarly, in his *From Sambo to Superspade: The Black Experience in Motion Pictures* (1975), Daniel J. Leab states that:

> Other actors tried, but largely failed, to alter the stereotypes that had so restricted Robeson. Eddie Anderson, for one, achieved considerable prominence in the late 1930s as [white comedian] Jack Benny's sassy valet-chauffeur, Rochester. He occasionally outsmarted his boss and was obviously no Uncle Tom, but Rochester was still a servant and there were limits to how far he could go.

Anderson's films with Benny include *Man about Town* (1939), *Buck Benny Rides Again* (1940), *Love Thy Neighbor* (1940),

Hattie McDaniel receives an Academy Award for her performance in *Gone with the Wind*, 1940

and *The Meanest Man in the World* (1943). He is also known for his television and radio shows with Benny and for such films as *Birth of the Blues* (1941) and *Cabin in the Sky* (1943).

World War II and the 1940s

In her own brilliant way, Hattie McDaniel had subtly changed the way in which blacks were viewed by moviegoers during the 1930s. Although typically cast as a maid or "mammy" to white families, she took every opportunity (through raised eyebrows, meaningful stares, and confidently delivered, often comic, lines that left no doubt of her opinions) to stress the underlying equality of the races. McDaniel perfected her

unique screen presence in such films as *Alice Adams* (1935), *Show Boat* (1936), *Saratoga* (1937), and *The Mad Miss Manton* (1938).

On the brink of World War II, David O. Selznick released a one-of-a-kind movie titled *Gone with the Wind* (1939), starring Clark Gable and Vivien Leigh. The film, set in the Civil War South, ranks as one of Hollywood's greatest pieces of entertainment. Hattie McDaniel was among the black actors in the cast, as were Eddie Anderson and Butterfly McQueen.

Giving the performance of a lifetime as Vivien Leigh's (Scarlett O'Hara's) wise, loving, and no-nonsense mammy, McDaniel finally drew the honor she deserved. In 1940 she received an Oscar—the first ever awarded to a black American—for best supporting actress. Whatever shortcomings the film's portrayal of blacks may have, McDaniel had triumphed personally, and paved the way for later celebrations of black artistry on screen.

The new liberalism of the World War II years, with a concern for morale at home and support of the country's armed forces, had a positive influence on the black's screen image. In such pictures as *Of Mice and Men* (1939) and *Strange Incident* (1943), blacks appeared as dignified, even heroic, figures. And fewer films glorified the Old South. The 1940s also saw growing vocal protest from the black and liberal press, and from such groups as the National Association for the Advancement of Colored People (NAACP) and the International Film and Radio Guild. Pressure from these sources did much to erase offensive dialogue and stereotypical roles.

Undoubtedly the biggest African American star of the decade was Lena Horne, who

Lena Horne in *Stormy Weather*

debuted in *Panama Hattie* (1942) and went on to star in the all-black musicals *Cabin in the Sky* (1943) and *Stormy Weather* (1943). Although Horne is perhaps better known for her later successes as a nightclub singer, recording artist, and Broadway star, she ranks as one of the most beautiful and talented film actresses of the era, and was the first black to sign a long-term contract with a major studio (MGM).

Dorothy Dandridge and the 1950s

Horne's successor during the 1950s was Dorothy Dandridge, who appeared in more than 25 films. In virtually all of her major pictures, the light-skinned Dandridge played a tragic mulatto, forever seeking but never finding happiness. Her most famous role was that of the title character in *Carmen Jones* (1954), an all-black musical that also starred Harry Belafonte.

Yet despite receiving an Academy Award nomination for best actress in this picture, Dandridge—much like her screen characters—faced limited opportunities because of her color. Extremely talented and a favorite of black audiences, she was never allowed to compete on the same level as the white film goddesses of the time (Marilyn Monroe and Jane Russell, for example). Yet in a string of pictures beginning with *Island in the Sun* (1957), she was able to break with a long-standing convention when she was romantically paired with white men. However, *Island in the Sun* was so controversial that the rest of her films dealing with interracial love were filmed overseas. One of Dandridge's last films was the traditional musical *Porgy and Bess* (1959), in which she was radiant alongside costar Sidney Poitier.

The Reign of Sidney Poitier

Poitier made his Hollywood debut in 1950 with the film *No Way Out,* the first of the "race problem" pictures that would characterize much of the 1950s and 1960s. He later distinguished himself in such films as *Cry the Beloved Country* (1952), *Blackboard Jungle* (1956), and *Edge of the City* (1957) before he starred in *The Defiant Ones* (1958) and became the first black man to be nominated for a best actor Oscar.

Seven years later Poitier not only was nominated for but won the best actor award for his performance as a laborer who befriends a group of nuns in *Lilies of the Field* (1964). This picture marked a turning point

Dorothy Dandridge and Harry Belafonte in *Carmen Jones*

in Poitier's career, for it prompted Hollywood to consider him for roles other than those specifically written for blacks. Within three short years, he would become one of the most popular film stars in America.

Following *To Sir with Love* (1967) and *In the Heat of the Night* (1967), Poitier starred alongside Katherine Houghton, Spencer Tracy, and Katharine Hepburn in *Guess Who's Coming to Dinner?* (1968). Poitier's

Sidney Poitier, the first black to win an Oscar for a starring role, in *Lilies of the Field*

plays a world-famous black doctor who has become engaged to a white girl who comes from a wealthy and fairly broad-minded family. Nonetheless, the engagement comes as a shock to both Poitier's and Houghton's parents.

Because Poitier was allowed only the briefest and tamest displays of affection for his fiancée, some considered the film to be cowardly, if not farcical. Others, who approached the film from a racist viewpoint, wanted the movie banned and led protests outside theaters that played it, particularly in the South. On the whole, though, the Ameri-

can public received the film warmly in the wake of the consciousness-raising civil rights movement. Yet Poitier himself soon faded from the big screen, making his most significant contributions in later years as a director.

Black Power, Black Direction, and Blaxploitation

When blacks began to assert themselves more stridently—through the example of Malcolm X—during the late 1960s, the film industry took note. *Up Tight* (1968) was based on the events in a major ghetto following the assassination of Martin Luther King,

Jr. And as blacks forged ahead in the film industry, Gordon Parks led a quiet revolution, becoming the first black to direct a film (*The Learning Tree,* 1969) for a major studio. Veteran actor Ossie Davis tried his hand at directing a year later with *Cotton Comes to Harlem* (1970), adapted from the novel by Chester Himes. The action comedy proved to be a smash box office hit and opened a busy decade of black-oriented films.

The tone of the decade was actually set the following year with the releases of Melvin Van Peebles's X-rated *Sweet Sweetback's Baadasssss Song* (1971) and Parks's *Shaft* (1971), starring Richard Roundtree. Both films were ground breaking, relying heavily on sex and violence and focusing upon a strong, supremely confident black hero. And both sparked the movie phenomenon that came to be known as blaxploitation.

A black film boom was quickly born: huge profits were available now that a large moviegoing public interested in the street life exploits (and exploitation) of black characters—many of them drug pushers and pimps—had been tapped. Soon more than 15 blacks had directed feature films for major studios or independent distributors, including *Super Fly* (1972) and two sequels to the detective thriller *Shaft.*

However popular these films were among young audiences, leaders of major black organizations found fault with the emphasis on violence, immorality, and antiheroes. Even in Hollywood, some 400 concerned black performers met to discuss the black image in contemporary films. The result was the formation of a group called the **Coalition** Against Blaxploitation. Its purpose was to meet with studio and indus-

Richard Roundtree

try union heads to improve the image of blacks on screen and their working lot in Hollywood as well.

One film that presumably would have met with the Coalition's approval was *Sounder* (1972), one of the standout movies of the decade and, according to Ted Sennett in the 1986 book *Great Hollywood Movies,* "one of the great films on the American family in general and the black experience in particular." *Sounder* starred Cicely Tyson and Paul Winfield, both of whom quickly emerged as leading black movie and television stars.

Comedy: The Hottest Trend of the 1980s

The black exploitation film boom virtually disappeared as fast as it had arrived.

Richard Pryor and Gene Wilder in *Silver Streak*

Some producers continued to release such low-budget projects for a while, but they were all rejected by theatergoers looking for something new and different.

If there were a new trend in popular movies it was reflected in a revival of the comedy. When Poitier and a young, tough-talking, hilarious street comic named Richard Pryor collaborated with a gallery of other major black actors in *Uptown Saturday Night* (1974), a new era of black involvement in films was launched. The film was only a modest box office success, but it led to separate career paths for the two principal players.

By 1980 Poitier and Pryor had reunited as director and actor in *Stir Crazy* and the results were predictably successful. Poitier had grown over the previous decades to become the most prominent black presence in the movie industry, and Pryor, by virtue of his role in *Silver Streak* (1976) and his incomparable stand-up performance in *Richard Pryor—Live in Concert* (1979), had become one of Hollywood's best box-office draws.

Two years after the release of *Stir Crazy,* a young comedian from the late-night TV show *Saturday Night Live* made his film debut in the action comedy *48 Hours* (1982). His name was Eddie Murphy. Although his next film, *Trading Places*

Eddie Murphy as Axel Foley, in *Beverly Hills Cop II*

(1983), was less than artistically successful due to a hackneyed plot, Murphy nevertheless showed he had immense comic range as well as charismatic appeal.

These traits were in full display in what remains his most memorable performance, that of detective Axel Foley in *Beverly Hills Cop* (1985). With this film, and its sequel, *Beverly Hills Cop II* (1987), Murphy became one of the decade's few superstars and a truly powerful Hollywood figure.

The Color Purple *Controversy*

Despite such successes, the 1980s were largely lacking in serious black-oriented film projects. A number of major dramatic performers, including James Earl Jones, Billy Dee Williams, Cicely Tyson, Morgan Freeman, and Diahann Carroll, were cast instead in films designed to appeal to general audiences. Perhaps the most notable of

these was *An Officer and a Gentleman* (1982), in which Louis Gossett, Jr., starred as a tough drill instructor and walked away with an Oscar for best supporting actor.

One black film that stood alone was *The Color Purple* (1985), a sprawling production that Steven Spielberg adapted from Alice Walker's Pulitzer Prize-winning novel. The controversy surrounding the movie centered around two issues: Spielberg's domineering direction and the seemingly antimale stance of Walker's narrative. A third issue, the fact that Spielberg was white, was perhaps also at stake.

Yet, according to a May 1992 article in *Ebony*, Walker herself ensured that the movie remain as much as possible not only a black, but a black female, production. Before filming began, she sought many concessions, including an agreement that at least half of the production crew be composed of black women. Sadly, the controversy carried over into the voting for the Academy Awards, negatively affecting a superb cast that included Danny Glover, Margaret Avery, and both Oprah Winfrey and Whoopi Goldberg in debut performances. Despite capturing 11 nominations, including those for best picture, best supporting actress (Margaret Avery and Oprah Winfrey), and best actress (Whoopi Goldberg), the film never received a single Oscar. Of course, Glover (in his *Lethal Weapon* roles), Winfrey (through her syndicated TV show and the TV movie *The Women of Brewster Place*), Goldberg (in her Oscar-winning supporting role in *Ghost*), and even Spielberg (in his best picture and best director Academy Awards for *Schindler's List*) have all ultimately prevailed.

Whoopi Goldberg and Margaret Avery in *The Color Purple*

Spike Lee and a New Era of Filmmaking

Two years after releasing *She's Gotta Have It,* Spike Lee produced a **seriocomic** musical titled *School Daze* (1988). The film met with only partial approval; among its several flaws, according to critics, were its one-dimensional female characters. Nonetheless, Lee emerged secure in his reputation as an **uncompromising** and inventive black filmmaker.

The film that solidified Lee's reputation (and prompted every Hollywood studio to seek its own maverick black director) was *Do the Right Thing* (1989), a story of a hot summer day in a black Brooklyn neighborhood and the events leading up to an outbreak of racial violence. Movie critic Roger Ebert called it "the most honest, complex and unblinking film I have ever seen about the subject of racism." The film that clinched Lee's hold upon the title "America's first black movie mogul" (a title given him in Alex Patterson's unauthorized biography) was *Malcolm X* (1992), which also ranks as his most controversial film to date.

Malcolm X

The making of *Malcolm X* became a per-

Spike Lee and Danny Aiello in a scene from Lee's *Do the Right Thing*

sonal mission for Lee, who had long been an admirer of the legendary black leader. He fought tooth and nail to win the right to direct the film and to defend his vision of Malcolm X. When he learned of Warner Bros. studio's plans to make the movie, Norman Jewison had already been chosen as its director. But after Lee told the *New York Times* that he had a "big problem" with a white man directing the film, Jewison agreed to bow out.

This was only the beginning of Lee's uphill battle. In addition to severe limitations on the money he could spend making the picture, as well as the related pressures of seeing the film through its final stages, Lee faced opposition from a group that called itself the United Front to Preserve the Memory of Malcolm X and the Cultural Revolution. Led by poet and activist Imamu Amiri Baraka (formerly LeRoi Jones), the group published an open letter, which said in part: "Our distress about Spike's making a film on Malcolm is based on our analysis of the [exploitative] films he has already made."

Against enormous odds, Lee finished the picture, though not without kicking in a portion of his own $3 million salary and also seeking additional funding from such black celebrities as Bill Cosby, Oprah Winfrey, Michael Jordan, Janet Jackson, and Prince—much to the studio's embarrassment.

Oscar winner Denzel Washington (center) in a scene from *Glory,* the 1989 film celebrating the heroic 54th Massachusetts Infantry regiment of the Civil War

Although *Malcolm X* received no Oscars, the film played a giant role in the elevation of the black leader to mythic status. It also spawned a phenomenon known as "Malcolm-mania." By the time the movie was released, its logo, a bold "X," was pasted on everything from baseball caps to posters, postcards, and T-shirts. Yet Lee is quick to defend himself against charges of **commercialism.** In fact, he says, Malcolm X's philosophy—that African Americans need to build their own economic base—is the reason for his business investments.

In the spring of 1993 Lee released his seventh feature film, *Crooklyn.* Set in 1970s Brooklyn and focusing on the Carmichael family of parents, four sons, and one daughter, *Crooklyn* is a comic, tender tribute to Lee's childhood.

John Singleton

Lee's breakthrough example was no doubt especially important to fellow filmmaker John Singleton, who in 1986 graduated from high school and entered the University of Southern California's Filmic Writing Program. By May 1990, Singleton had polished the script for *Boyz N the Hood* and sent it to Columbia Pictures. Columbia wanted to make the picture, but at first

John Singleton

wanted someone else to direct it. Singleton believed only he could do it.

Columbia finally agreed and budgeted $7 million for the project. The result was a singularly powerful movie, which probed more deeply and effectively into a portion of black society than had any previous film. Unfortunately, on July 12, 1991, the film opened to violence in and around theaters. Shootings and knifings left 2 dead and more than 30 injured in incidents at about 20 theaters from Los Angeles to Chicago to Detroit. In response, 21 of the 829 theaters showing the film decided to drop it. Singleton labeled this response "artistic racism."

No convincing argument has been offered to show a link between the film and the violence that accompanied its opening. Indeed, the purpose of the film was not to promote violence, but to offer a peaceful solution (the film's motto was "Increase the Peace"). For his efforts, Singleton received an Academy Award nomination for best director, thus becoming the first African American and the youngest person ever to be so honored. In the summer of 1993, Singleton released his second film, *Poetic Justice,* starring Janet Jackson. It received favorable reviews.

The New Era Questioned

The year *Boyz* was released a virtual boom in black films occurred. In all, a record 19 black-oriented films made it to movie theaters, including *The Five Heartbeats, Straight out of Brooklyn, New Jack City, Jungle Fever, Up against the Wall, Strictly Business, Chameleon Street, Livin' Large,* and *House Party 2.* By this time, most were willing to acknowledge that a black film renaissance—more important and valuable than that of the 1970s—was firmly underway.

However, in an essay on black directors for Peter Rainer's *Love and Hisses* (1992), Carrie Rickey found at least one industry figure, *Rage in Harlem* director Bill Duke, who remains pessimistic. Duke denies that a black film renaissance has arrived because:

In the context of the entire industry, what's happening now is only a small step. In Hollywood, there are still no African-American executives who can greenlight a project. In the realm of distribution, there is no African-American-controlled entity. In marketing, there is no one. And in exhibition, there is only one first-run theater in the entire country, the Baldwin (in Los Angeles), that is African-American owned.

Julie Dash

Julie Dash

One might add that there is only one black woman director, Julie Dash, who has brought a feature-length film to a nationwide audience. Her *Daughters of the Dust* (1992) focuses on a family of Gullahs—blacks of West African descent living on islands off the southeastern coast of the United States— at the dawn of the twentieth century.

Dash's first creative film work (she began her career in **documentary** film) was *Diary of an African Nun* (1977), an adaptation of a short story by Alice Walker. The literature of notable black women authors played a major role in Dash's decision to become involved with creative film. "I stopped making documentaries after discovering Toni Morrison, Toni Cade Bambara, and Alice Walker," she explained to the *Village Voice*. "I'd wondered, why can't we see movies like this? I realized I needed to learn how to make narrative movies."

It remains to be seen whether other black women will soon follow Dash's lead, though *House Party* director Warrington Hudlin speculates that television directors Debbie Allen and Neema Barnett, who have worked on *A Different World* and *The Cosby Show,* may be among the likeliest candidates.

Whatever the future of black film in America, it is clear that the recent surge of public demand, Hollywood backing, and fresh on-screen and behind-the-camera talent has greatly enriched the entertainment industry as a whole.

FACT FOCUS

- Timmie Rogers, sometimes called "the dean of black comedians," launched the first all-black show, *Sugar Hill Times,* in 1948 on CBS television.
- Hazel Dorothy Scott was the first black performer to have her own network television program, from 1948 to 1950.
- In 1963 Cicely Tyson became the first black to appear in a key part on a television series (*East Side, West Side*).
- In 1965 Bill Cosby broke the color barrier in television when he became the first black to star in a network series, *I Spy.* Three years later, Diahann Carroll starred in her own situation comedy (sitcom) *Julia* (1968-71).
- The first black television show sponsored by a black business was *Soul Train.*
- The longest-running black series in the history of television was *The Jeffersons,* which began in 1975 and ran through 1985.
- *Roots* scored the highest ratings in television history when it aired for eight consecutive days in January 1977.
- In 1989 Arsenio Hall became the first black man to host a nationally broadcast television talk show. This same year, Jennifer Lawson became the highest ranking black woman executive in public television.
- An outspoken critic of black images in television, Cosby made a unsuccessful bid on October 28, 1992, to purchase the National Broadcasting Company (NBC).
- A decade before Cosby began to make his mark, the state of black-oriented television was dismal. Except for a handful of black variety shows, networks offered little that directly touched black audiences. One program, CBS's *Amos 'N' Andy,* was adapted from the tremendously popular radio series and aired from 1951 to 1953. Although the show attracted a sizeable following, it was canceled after black organizations protested against its stereotyped portrayals of African Americans. Reruns of the show continued until 1966, when pressure from civil rights leaders convinced CBS to take the show out of circulation entirely.
- For countless viewers of all races and ages, Bill Cosby represents the essence of entertaining television. And this is particularly fitting, for Cosby has been a pioneer television performer from his first days on the set of *I Spy* (1965-68) until the final episode of *The Cosby Show,* which aired in 1992.

TELEVISION
I Spy

During the thick of the civil rights movement, a television producer named Sheldon Leonard (already credited with *The Andy Griffith Show, Gomer Pyle,* and *The Dick Van Dyke Show*) decided the time was ripe for a black television lead; he approached Bill Cosby, a rising stand-up comedian.

Cosby was to star alongside Robert Culp in a show about two globetrotting CIA agents, one (Culp) posing as a tennis player and the other (Cosby) as his trainer. Of the two, Cosby would be the "brains," an Oxford-educated Rhodes scholar.

Although the show was well-conceived, according to Robert Rosenberg in *Bill Cosby: The Changing Black Image,* (1991):

Bill Cosby with costar Robert Culp on the set of *I Spy*

NBC was especially nervous that southern stations might refuse to carry the show, and that some advertisers would pull their commercials rather than have their products associated with a controversial program. A final problem was that Cosby had no professional acting experience.

By the end of the season, however, all of the network's fears had been put to rest. The show was a hit and Cosby was honored with an Emmy—the first of three—for best actor in a dramatic series. Following *I Spy,* Cosby kept his hand in television with two less successful programs, *The Bill Cosby Show* (1969-71) and *Cos* (1976); he was also involved with the public television children's show *The Electric Company* and the highly successful *Fat Albert and the Cosby Kids* (1972-77) Saturday morning cartoon series. *Fat Albert* was the first show of its kind to feature blacks as its main characters. Of course, Cosby would surface again in the 1980s with one of television's all-time megahits.

The 1970s and the Rise of Programs for Blacks

While Cosby and Diahann Carroll (as star of the series *Julia*) were making television history during the late 1960s, another black performer was becoming more and more familiar to mainstream America. His name was Redd Foxx.

A raunchy, irresistible comedian, Foxx was one of the top stars of the comedy circuit and was getting requests to appear in guest spots on some of the most popular television shows of the time, including

Redd Foxx achieved national attention with *Sanford and Son*

Here's Lucy, The Addams Family, Green Acres, Mr. Ed, and *The Lucy Show.* Then, in 1970, he appeared in Ossie Davis's film *Cotton Comes to Harlem.*

Sanford and Son

Although his part as an elderly junk dealer was small, his performance was good enough to catch the eye of television producers Bud Yorkin and Norman Lear. On January 14, 1972, *Sanford and Son,* starring Foxx as an ornery junk dealer from Watts, premiered to rave reviews. For most of its five-year run, *Sanford and Son* ranked among the top ten programs on television, bringing Foxx a Golden Globe Award as well as four Emmy nominations. The show's popularity also earned Foxx one of

Flip Wilson

son. His *The Flip Wilson Show* (1970-74) was the first comedy-variety program to star a black performer. He immediately became famous for such original character creations as "Geraldine" and "The Reverend Leroy." In 1976 Wilson made his dramatic television debut on the series *The Six Million Dollar Man.*

Good Times

Good Times (1974-79) began as a spinoff from the series *Maude,* in which Esther Rolle portrayed maid Florida Evans. A pioneering show of black urban life that was both serious and comic, *Good Times* revolved around the Evans family and was set in the Cabrini-Green Housing Project in Chicago. Until 1976 John Amos played Florida's husband. (Amos had earlier portrayed Gordy the weatherman on the *Mary Tyler Moore Show* and later starred as the adult Kunta Kinte in *Roots.* In the spring of 1994 the sit-com *704 Hauser*—a take-off on *All in the Family*—premiered, with Amos in the lead.)

But the true star of *Good Times* was comedian Jimmie Walker in his role as the eldest son of the Evanses, "J. J." Walker's lovable antics, get-rich-quick schemes, and trademark phrase "Dyn-o-mite!" captured the imaginations of millions of viewers and catapulted the series to the top of the list during its opening season. In 1977 Rolle left the show after a dispute over the character of "J. J." and the poor image of blacks that he represented. She eventually returned after the show's producers agreed to make certain changes, but by then the show's ratings had plunged too far to recover.

The Jeffersons

The next major black show to air was

the highest salaries paid to a television star at the time—close to $35,000 an episode.

Like Cosby, Foxx followed up his initial success with a few failed shows (*The Redd Foxx Comedy Hour,* 1977-78; *Sanford,* 1980-81; and *The Redd Foxx Show,* 1986) before landing another potential hit, *The Royal Family* (1991-92), with costar Della Reese. But on October 11, 1991, during a brief rehearsal for the show, Foxx made his final exit as he slumped to the floor with a heart attack; he died hours later.

The Flip Wilson Show

Even more visible than Foxx, at least during the early 1970s, was comedian Flip Wil-

John Amos, Esther Rolle, and Jimmie Walker in a scene from *Good Times*

another spinoff (from *All in the Family*) titled *The Jeffersons*. From 1975 to 1985 former neighbors of working-class white bigot Archie Bunker—George (Sherman Hemsley) and Louise (Isabel Sanford) Jefferson—were "movin' on up" thanks to the success of George's dry-cleaning business and Louise's wise and tempering influence (George was himself a bigot and prone to making rash decisions).

The Jeffersons was a trend-setting black show in a number of ways. First, it ran for 11 seasons and thus ranks as the longest-running black show in television history. Second, it depicted for the first time a wealthy black family. And third, it introduced a biracial couple to American viewers. Although Hemsley, in his gruff, imperfect, and humorous manner defined the series, Marla Gibbs (as wisecracking maid Florence) was equally outstanding.

Among the many other black shows of the 1970s that vied for America's attention were *That's My Mama* (1974-75), *What's*

The cast of *The Jeffersons,* starring (bottom center) Isabel Sanford and Sherman Hemsley

Happening (1976-79), and *Diff'rent Strokes* (1978-86), the latter more an unrealistic vehicle for young comedian Gary Coleman than a show about black life.

Roots

Although comedy reigned king during the 1970s, a handful of dramatic television movies about blacks were highly successful. One of the most notable was the two-hour film *Autobiography of Miss Jane Pittman* (1974), which starred Cicely Tyson and was nominated for nine (and received two) Emmy Awards.

But there was one dramatic project that stood out above all the rest, *Roots,* inspired by Alex Haley's novel of the same title. The miniseries, presented over eight nights, captivated some 130 million viewers during its run and became the most talked about black program of the decade.

A dramatization of Haley's own African ancestry, *Roots* was praised for much more than its entertainment value. It was, above all, a door leading directly into the whole African American experience. National Urban League director Vernon Jordan described *Roots* as "the single most spectacular education experience in race relations in America." In addition, the program served as a symbol of black pride and hope that television might shift its programming to depict more aspects of the black experience in America.

Prominent among the large cast were LeVar Burton (better known to younger viewers as Lieutenant Geordi LaForge in *Star Trek: The Next Generation,* 1987-94), Ben Vereen, Leslie Uggams, Louis Gossett, Jr., Cicely Tyson, and Richard Roundtree. A sequel, *Roots: The Next Generation,* appeared in 1979 over the course of seven nights. Although not quite as popular as the original miniseries (which scored the highest ratings in television history for an entertainment program), the sequel defeated some heavy competition, winning each of its time slots and attracting an overall audience of 110 million.

A number of black television specials followed in the wake of *Roots,* including films on the lives of Martin Luther King, Jr., Harriet Tubman, Olympic gold medalist Wilma Rudolph, and baseball great Satchel Paige. Yet there was no carryover to a regular, prime-time dramatic series centered on African Americans. These would be forthcoming during the 1980s (for example, *Paris* with James Earl Jones and *The Lazarus Syndrome* with Louis Gossett, Jr.), though evidently doomed to a short life.

The 1980s

Meanwhile, the sitcom success of *The Jeffersons* continued. The season after the show

The cast of *The Cosby Show,* 1987

concluded, Sherman Hemsley found himself again starring in another popular black series, *Amen,* which ran from 1986 to 1991. Around the same time, Marla Gibbs became the star of her own series, *227* (1985-90), which was paired with *Amen* on NBC. The show that led NBC to prime-time dominance during the 1980s, however, was the Thursday-night leadoff hit *The Cosby Show.*

The Cosby Show

Interestingly, no one except perhaps Cosby, the show's creator, imagined how successful it would be. In a near replay of the situation that faced Cosby during the 1960s, network executives still worried that there were racial limitations to what mainstream, and even black, audiences wanted to

The cast of *In Living Color*, 1991

see on television. According to Robert Rosenberg, these executives:

> Feared that no one would want to watch a situation comedy about an upper-middle class black family that was comfortable with its status [George Jefferson, during his 11 seasons, was anything but comfortable]. Both blacks and whites might resent the good fortune of the characters on the show. Viewers might think the show did not represent the way things really were.

But Cosby persisted. His character, an obstetrician named Heathcliff Huxtable, broke with all the stereotypes. He was warm, witty, comical, highly competent (except when it came to home improvement projects), moderately wealthy, a loving husband and father, and, above all, a playful child at heart.

The show quickly soared to the number one position. And throughout its life, it remained consistently among the ten most popular shows on television. Although Cosby was unmistakably the center of attention, Phylicia Rashad, Lisa Bonet, Malcolm-Jamal Warner, Tempestt Bledsoe, Keshia Knight Pulliam, and Sabrina LeBeauf were all essential to the show's enormous appeal.

In 1987 *A Different World,* a spinoff starring college-age Lisa Bonet (Denise Huxtable) aired. Although the show never met with the same critical success, it was still highly popular and ran until 1993. Bonet herself departed after the second season, leaving room for Jasmine Guy (as Southern belle Whitley Gilbert) and a number of other black actors to achieve stardom.

Current Programming

During the 1990s, as in previous decades, sitcoms dominated black programming. Among the prominent shows during the 1993-94 season were *The Fresh Prince of Bel-Air,* starring rapper and actor (*Six Degrees of Separation*) Will "Fresh Prince" Smith; *Roc,* with Charles Dutton; *Thea,* with comic Thea Vidale; *Sister, Sister,* with Tim Reid, Jackee Harry, and Tamera and Tia Mowry; *South Central,* starring Larenz Tate and Tasha Scott; *Living Single,* with Kim Fields, Kim Coles, Erika Alexander, and Queen Latifah; and *In Living Color,* an irreverent variety show created by star Keenan Ivory Wayans and also featuring his siblings Damon, Shawn, and Kim. Of these, only *South Central,* a Fox program about a single mother raising three children in poverty-ridden south central Los Angeles, was created for anything more than light-hearted entertainment.

Rosalind Bentley, a television critic for the *Minneapolis Star Tribune,* reviewed the fall lineup with an article meaningfully headed "Get Serious: New Black TV Shows Are Same Old Simplistic Stuff" (October 3, 1993). In the article, she posed the question: "Where is the balance? Where is the totality of black life on television?" If there is to be a change, she concludes, it must come from black viewers willing to speak out for their likes and dislikes. "I've heard many a friend grumble about how silly *Martin* [for example] makes black folks look, but not one of us has written to a production company or studio to voice those concerns."

21
Media

The African American
Press and Broadcast Media

"I am grateful and blessed because those women whose names made the history books, and a lot who did not, are all bridges that I've crossed over to get to this side."—*Oprah Winfrey*

Black participation and influence in America's print and broadcast **media** has increased since 30, and even 20, years ago. These strides include an increase in the number of black-operated and oriented radio stations; a rise in the major television networks and local **affiliates** featuring black-themed programs such as *Tony Brown's Journal;* more locally hosted public affairs programs such as Gil Noble's *Positively Black* on New York's ABC-TV; and the debut of Black Entertainment Television. African Americans also successfully challenged biased programming and employment by television and radio stations.

In addition, the number of black journalists and commentators employed by general interest newspapers and broadcasters increased. Nationally **syndicated** columnist Carl Rowan continued to be heard on a number of radio stations across the country

and other columnists such as William Raspberry, Tony Brown, Les Payne, and Robert Maynard have become household names throughout the United States.

During this period, there was also an explosion of special interest magazines catering to blacks. These included *Essence* and *Black Enterprise,* which have also attracted a sizeable white audience.

Newspaper and Magazine Publishers

Newspapers

The modern African American press is heir to a great, largely unheralded tradition. It began with the first black newspaper, *Freedom's Journal,* edited and published by Samuel Cornish and John B. Russwurm, on March 16, 1827. *North Star,* the newspaper of abolitionist Frederick Douglass, was first published on December 3, 1847.

By the 1880s the ability of blacks to establish a substantial cultural environment in many cities of the North led to the creation of a new wave of publications, includ-

The black press in America goes back to 1827, when Samuel Cornish and John B. Russwurm began publishing *Freedom's Journal*

ing the *Washington Bee, Indianapolis World, Philadelphia Tribune, Cleveland Gazette, Baltimore Afro-American,* and *New York Age.* By 1900 daily papers appeared in Norfolk, Kansas City, and Washington, D.C.

Among famous black newspaper editors were William Monroe Trotter, editor of the *Boston Guardian,* a self-styled "radical" paper that opposed Booker T. Washington's trade-based program for black advancement; Robert S. Abbott, whose *Chicago Defender* pioneered the use of headlines and

became the most widely circulated black weekly by the 1940s; and T. Thomas Fortune of the *New York Age,* who championed free public schools in an age when many opposed the idea.

The National Negro Newspaper Publishers Association

The National Negro Newspaper Publishers Association was founded in 1940, at a time when there were more than 200 black newspapers and about 120 black magazines

John Henry Murphy founded the *Baltimore Afro-American* in 1892

in the country. The organization scheduled workshops and trips abroad to acquaint editors and reporters with important news centers and news sources. A trend to more progressive and **interpretive** reporting resulted. In 1956 the association changed its name to the National Newspaper Publishers Association; today it represents around 150 publishers.

The Amsterdam News

Founded in 1909 in New York City by James H. Anderson, the *Amsterdam News* has become one of the most well-known black newspapers in the nation. During its early days, the *Amsterdam News* had a staff of ten and the paper, which consisted of six printed pages, sold for just two cents a copy.

In 1935 the paper was sold to two black physicians, Clilan B. Powell and P. M. H. Savory. In 1971 the paper was again sold to a group of investors, headed by Clarence B. Jones and Percy E. Sutton.

Black Newspapers in the 1990s

A number of newspapers that began publishing in the 1960s, 1970s, and 1980s have gone out of business due to declining advertising revenues and other factors. Yet, until 1975 there was only one major black daily newspaper, *The Chicago Defender.* There are now three, the *Defender, The Atlanta Daily World,* and *The Daily Challenge,* published in Brooklyn, New York. In all, there are a reported 214 black newspapers in the United States. Of these, the papers with the largest paid circulations include New York's *Black American,* the *Hartford Inquirer,* and the *Atlanta Voice.*

Magazines

As early as the 1830s black magazines were being published in the United States. It was not until the 1900s, however, that the first truly successful magazines appeared. In 1910 the National Association for the Advancement of Colored People (NAACP) began publishing *Crisis,* under the editorship of W. E. B. Du Bois. By the end of the decade, some 100,000 copies of the magazine were in print. In November 1942, John H. Johnson launched the *Negro Digest,* an instantly successful periodical containing both news reprints and feature articles.

Within three years Johnson was ready with another magazine, patterned after *Life* and titled *Ebony.* Its first print run of 25,000 copies sold out immediately. Today *Ebony* has a circulation rate of almost 2,000,000.

1827 The first black newspaper, *Freedom's Journal,* is launched by Samuel Cornish and John Russwurm.

1892 Ida B. Wells-Barnett, remembered as the first black woman journalist, becomes co-owner of the *Memphis Free Speech* and continues her campaign against lynching.

1944 Harry McAlpin of Atlanta's *Daily World* becomes the first African American White House news reporter.

1949 Gordon Parks, Sr., becomes the first black photojournalist on the staff of *Life* magazine.

1958 Joan Murray becomes the first major black television news correspondent.

1978 Charlayne Hunter-Gault becomes the first black woman to **anchor** a national newscast.

1986 Oprah Winfrey becomes the first African American woman to host a nationally **syndicated** weekday talk show.

1989 Clarence Page, a writer for the *Chicago Tribune,* becomes the first black columnist to be awarded a Pulitzer Prize.

1993 Delano Eugene Lewis is named president of National Public Radio and becomes the first black to head a major public broadcasting organization.

AFRICAN AMERICAN ANTISLAVERY NEWSPAPERS

Title	City	Established
Freedom's Journal	New York, New York	March 30, 1827
Rights of All	New York, New York	March 28, 1828
Weekly Advocate	New York, New York	January 1837
Colored American (formerly Weekly Advocate)	New York, New York	March 4, 1837
Elevator	Albany, New York	1842
National Watchman	Troy, New York	1842
Clarion		1842
People's Press	New York, New York	1843
Mystery	Pittsburgh, Pennsylvania	1843
Genius of Freedom		1845
Ram's Horn	New York, New York	January 1, 1847
North Star	Rochester, New York	November 1, 1847
Moral Reform Magazine	Philadelphia, Pennsylvania	1847
Impartial Citizen	Syracuse, New York	1848
Christian Herald	Philadelphia, Pennsylvania	1848
Colored Man's Journal	New York, New York	1851
Alienated American	Cleveland, Ohio	1852
Christian Recorder (formerly Christian Herald)	Philadelphia, Pennsylvania	1852
Mirror of the Times	San Francisco, California	1855
Herald of Freedom	Ohio	1855
Anglo African	New York, New York	July 23, 1859

Sources: Rayford W. Logan and Michael R. Winston, editors *Dictionary of American Negro Biography,* Norton, 1983, pp. 134-35, 538-39; *Negro Yearbook,* 1913, *p. 75;* I. Garland *Penn, The Afro-American Press and Its Editors,* 1891, reprint, Ayer, 1969.

In 1950 Johnson launched the magazine *Tan,* followed by *Jet* in 1951. Like *Ebony* and *Negro Digest, Jet* was an instant success, selling over 300,000 copies in its first year. *Tan,* a woman's magazine, was later transformed into a show business and personality monthly called *Black Stars.*

Since the founding of *Ebony,* several new and specialized black magazines have appeared. In 1967 *Black American Litera-*

Gordon Parks, Sr.

black middle class. Today *Black Enterprise* has a subscription rate of over 251,000.

Essence, a magazine founded in 1970 and directed at black women, has steadily gained in its circulation since its start. Featuring health and beauty, fashion, and contemporary living sections, *Essence* is considered to be one of the top women's magazines. Susan Taylor serves as the magazine's editor in chief.

In 1980 *Black Family,* a magazine promoting positive lifestyles for African Americans, was founded. In 1986 *American Visions,* the official magazine of the African American Museums Association, was first published.

In 1993 there were a reported 61 black magazines in the United States. Of these, only *Ebony* had a circulation of more than 1 million. *Jet* trailed with 968,545 and *Essence* followed with 850,116.

ture Review, a journal presenting essays, interviews, poems, and book reviews, was founded. Also in 1967 Project Magazines, Inc. began publishing *Black Careers.* In 1969 the Black World Foundation published the first edition of *The Black Scholar.*

Earl G. Graves, a young businessman, decided in 1970 to publish a monthly digest of news, commentary, and informative articles for blacks interested in business. Within a few short years his *Black Enterprise* was accepted as the authority on African Americans in business and as an important supporter of an active, socially responsive

Broadcasting

Before there was a broadcast industry there were black journalists. But in the Jim Crow America of the 1920s, there had to be black-oriented radio before there could be black broadcast journalists. That mission fell to a jack-of-all trades from Cincinnati, Jack L. Cooper (1888-1970).

Radio

While early radio shows featured black singing groups, they featured no blacks talking; to Cooper, this "was like taxation without representation." On Sunday, November 3, 1929, at 5 P.M., Chicago's white-owned WSBC premiered *The All-Negro Hour,* starring Cooper and friends. Born was the concept of black radio, and Cooper went on to become the nation's first black radio station executive, the first black newscaster, the first black sportscaster, and the first to use radio as a service medium.

Cooper wore many hats. He played second base for a semi-pro baseball team and was a singer, dancer, and **vaudeville** performer. He fought 160 amateur boxing bouts and he managed theaters. Between about 1910 and 1924 he worked as a journalist, writing for a number of black newspapers, including the *Freeman, Ledger,* and *Recorder* in Indianapolis and the *Bluff City News* and *Western World Reporter* in Memphis. In 1924 he became the assistant theatrical editor of the *Chicago Defender.*

The All-Negro Hour was like a vaudeville revue on the air, featuring music, comedy, and serials. After the show ended its run in 1935, Cooper continued with WSBC, pioneering the black-radio format by producing several black-oriented shows. Crucial to that format was local news and public affairs of interest to African Americans.

The first example of public service programming aired December 9, 1938, when Cooper launched the *Search for Missing Persons* show. Aimed at reuniting people who had lost contact with friends and relatives through migration and over time, it reportedly had reunited 20,000 people by 1950. According to *Ebony* magazine, Cooper also remodeled a van into a mobile unit to relay "on-the-spot news events directly to four radio stations in the Chicago and suburban area," including news flashes from the *Pittsburgh Courier* and interviews of famous personalities who came to town, such as boxer Joe Louis. Cooper also did play-by-

play sportscasts of black baseball games from the van.

Listen Chicago, a news talk show that ran from 1946 to 1952, provided African Americans with their first opportunity to use radio as a public forum. Following Cooper's lead, between 1946 and 1955 the number of black oriented stations jumped from 24 to 600. News was a part of the explosion. "We have learned to do newscasts that answer the question, 'How is this news going to affect me as a Negro?,'" Leonard Walk of WHOD Pittsburgh said in 1954. "We have learned that church and social news deserves a unique place of importance in our daily Negro programming."

Yet by and large these broadcasters were not trained journalists. Black stations did not begin to broadcast news as we know it today until the 1960s.

In 1972 the Mutual Black Network was formed for news and sports syndication. By the end of the 1970s the Mutual Black Network had just over 100 affiliates and 6.2 million listeners. The Sheridan Broadcasting Corporation, a black-owned broadcasting chain based in Pittsburgh, purchased the Mutual Black Network in the late 1970s, renaming it the Sheridan Broadcasting Network. A second African American radio network, the National Black Network, was formed in 1973. Among its regular features was commentary by journalist Roy Wood. It has since gone out of business. In January 1992 the American Urban Radio Network was formed.

The networks were a mixed blessing. They provided their affiliates with broadcast-quality programs produced from a black perspective. But this relatively inexpensive

CONSERVATIVE
AFRICAN AMERICAN RADIO PERSONALITIES

In the early 1990s there has been a trend in broadcasting toward promoting conservative African American talk-show hosts. These conservatives, such as Ken Hamblin of Denver's KNUS-AM, Armstrong Williams of Washington, D.C.'s WOL-AM, and Alan Keyes of Baltimore's WCBM-AM, challenge the long-held opinions of traditional African American political leaders and many African Americans.

With national polls showing trends toward conservatism on crime and on abortion, divorce, and other issues concerning the family, the message of the radio personalities—that African Americans should be self-reliant, and not expect the national government to solve their problems—has attracted listeners. Yet some liberal black radio personalities, including Clayton Riley of New York's WLIB, maintain that the conservatives' shows only hurt African Americans by providing racist whites with ammunition to use against them. The radio producers are "chasing the money to be made off hate," Riley is quoted as saying in *USA Weekend.* "They've learned it's a product you can sell. These aren't programs for the African community; they're underwritten [financed] by conservative think tanks."

But in an industry where personalities sometimes mean as much as politics and controversy always means higher ratings, look for a continuation of this trend.

Source: Jim Kennelly, "Radio's Rising Black Conservatives: Syndicated Talk Show Hosts' Views on Racial Politics Rattle the Liberal Establishment," *USA Weekend,* April 1-3, 1994, p. 16.

access to news, sports, and public affairs features discouraged the local stations that subscribed from producing their own shows. News and public affairs staffs at the black-oriented stations remained minimal. There were some notable exceptions, however.

New York's WLIB-AM had a black format that included a highly acclaimed news and public affairs department. A series of shows produced by the station on disadvantaged youth in the city won two Peabody Awards for excellence in journalism in 1970. After the station was purchased in 1972 by civic leader Percy Sutton, the station became "Your Total Black News and Information Station," offering more news and public affairs programming than any other black-formatted radio outlet in the country.

In Washington, D.C., *The Washington Post* donated its commercial FM radio license to Howard University in 1971. The new station, WHUR-FM, began *The Daily Drum,* an hour-long evening newscast that featured special coverage of the local as well as global black communities.

Television

Until the late 1960s most serious black journalists were in print journalism rather than broadcasting. An exception was Lionel Monagas, who worked in the early 1950s as a director of CBS-TV network programs such as *Person to Person* and *Face the Nation.*

In 1956 Monagas became the first black professional at public station Channel 35 in Philadelphia, later known as WHYY-TV. He produced several children's programs there, including a ten-part series *The History of the Negro,* narrated by Ossie Davis.

In 1962 Mal Goode became the first African American network television reporter. According to Goode, baseball great Jackie Robinson had something to do with this breakthrough. Complaining to an ABC vice president, Robinson said that the only two Negroes he had seen at ABC were "a lady with a white uniform in the lobby dusting and a Negro doorman." According to Goode, the vice president's "face got red, and he said we intend to do something about that."

Goode was a reporter at *The Pittsburgh Courier* at the time, but in 1949 Pittsburgh's KQV-Radio had given the newspaper two 15-minute slots to fill on Tuesday and Wednesday nights. Goode read the news on the program. According to Goode, ABC

chose him for the job after spending half a year interviewing 38 black male candidates. One reason he was chosen, he said, was because he was considered dark enough so blacks would know he was black, but light enough so that whites wouldn't feel threatened. Goode went on to work for ABC for 11 years. In addition to serving as ABC's United Nations correspondent, he covered the Cuban missile crisis, the aftermath of Martin Luther King, Jr.'s assassination, and the Poor People's March on Washington.

Jobs like Goode's were hard to come by. In his memoir *Black Is the Color of My TV Tube,* Emmy-winner Gil Noble of New York's WABC-TV recalls being at WLIB-AM radio during this era:

> We would sit in the newsroom and fantasize about earning $300 a week, but few of our number worked at that level. Pat Connell, a former disc jockey at Newark's WNJR, known as "Pat the Cat," was anchoring the CBS morning newscast. Mal Goode was reporting for ABC-TV news, as well as for the local station WABC. NBC didn't have any blacks at that time, as far as I can recall, and in the mid-'60s, WNEW-TV had none, nor did WPIX-TV or WOR-TV have any.

Noble recalled that when he went downtown to audition for a major radio station job, he would present "a [Walter] Cronkite delivery that outdid the original," only to get the familiar brushoff, "Thanks very much. You're fine, but we already have a Negro on staff."

However, a few blacks were allowed on the white-controlled airwaves. William C. Matney, Jr., who had been managing editor

Ed Bradley

of the *Michigan Chronicle* and a reporter for the *Detroit News,* in 1963 became a television and radio reporter for WMAQ-TV, the NBC-owned station in Chicago. He joined NBC-TV news in 1966. Veteran Norma Quarles, now at CNN, was hired as a trainee at NBC News in 1966, moving a year later to the NBC station in Cleveland as a reporter and **anchor.** Lem Tucker joined NBC News as a copy boy in 1965 and moved up to assistant bureau chief in Vietnam.

In 1967 a self-described "teacher moonlighting as a jazz disc jockey" who also called play-by-play for basketball games and read the news applied for a job at soon-to-be all-news WCBS radio in New York. Ed Bradley, who would later co-host CBS-TV's most successful news show, *60 Minutes,* impressed a news director by refusing to write some copy to record it. "You won't learn enough about me that way," Bradley explained to his potential employer; instead, he borrowed a tape recorder, went out on the street, did an update of a story about an antipoverty program, and got the job.

But in 1964 in Portsmouth, Virginia, a bold 25-year-old newscaster named Max Robinson was fired from a UHF station after he broke the rules by showing his face on camera. In 1971, however, Robinson became the first black anchor in a major market, at WTOP-TV in Washington, D.C. Finally, in 1978, at ABC-TV, Robinson became the networks' first black regular coanchor.

It took the riots of the 1960s and a stern warning from a federal commission for the broadcast industry to undertake any concentrated hiring of African Americans. When American cities began to burn, blacks held about 3.6 percent of television news jobs. White news directors had to scramble to find black journalists to cover the story. In 1968 the National Advisory Commission on Civil Disorders, known as the Kerner Commission, concluded that "the world that television and newspapers offer to their black audience is almost totally white, in both appearance and attitude." "Within a year," wrote Noble, "many of us found ourselves working downtown at major radio and TV stations."

In June 1969 the Federal Communications Commission (FCC) adopted rules barring discrimination in broadcast industry employment and required stations to file annual reports showing the racial makeup of

Bryant Gumbel interviews former president Richard Nixon, 1990

their workforce by job category. Black public-affairs shows were aired, such as Noble's *Like It Is,* Public Broadcasting's *Black Journal* hosted by Tony Brown, and Philadelphia's *Black Perspectives on the News,* in nearly every city with a large black population. Still, by the time Mal Goode retired in 1973 there were only seven black reporters at the three networks.

By the 1990s African Americans were breaking into broadcast management and ownership, though the numbers were still small. Television station general managers included Charlotte Moore English of

KSHB-TV in Kansas City; Marcellus Alexander of WJZ-TV in Baltimore; Eugene Lothery of WCAU-TV in Philadelphia; Clarence McKee, CEO and chairman of WTVT-TV in Tampa; and Dorothy Brunson, owner of a small UHF station, WGTW-TV, in Philadelphia.

Ronald Townsend, president of the Gannett Television Group, chaired the National Association of Broadcasters' television board. Jonathan Rodgers became president of the CBS Television Stations Division in August 1990, making him network TV's highest-ranking African American news executive. NBC *Today* show co-host Bryant Gumbel, CBS-News correspondent Ed Bradley, and talk-show host Oprah Winfrey became three of the highest paid and most recognized people on television. ABC-TV's Carole Simpson became a substitute and weekend network television anchor. And African Americans were anchoring local newscasts in markets around the country.

Nevertheless, although blacks make up 12 percent of the population in the 1990 census, African Americans represented only 9.8 percent of the television news workforce and 5 percent of the radio workforce. They represented 4 percent of the news directors at commercial television stations and about 5 percent at commercial radio stations. Those heading news operations included Gary Wordlaw at WJLA-TV in Washington, D.C., and Will Wright at WWOR-TV in New York. And according to an annual survey by the Center for Media and Public Affairs, most of the news on nightly network television shows continued to be presented by white males. Blacks accounted for only 5 percent of all field reports and anchor

Emmy Award-winning talk show host Oprah Winfrey

stories combined, its 1991 survey found. The most visible African American correspondent was George Strait, ABC-TV health reporter, who tied for fifty-seventh in the number of stories filed. Simpson was in sixth place, based on the number of brief news reports read.

Public Television

For most of its short history, public television, begun in the early 1950s, failed to realize the hopes of many African Americans. Tony Brown's *Black Journal* (later *Tony Brown's Journal*) was well-received by black viewers as the only national black public affairs series on television. It was constantly threatened with cancellation, however, after many complained about its anti-administration attitude. The show was rescued after it secured sponsorship from Pepsi Cola.

In 1975 the only black FCC commissioner, Benjamin Hooks, joined the critics, accusing public broadcasters of "arrogance" and of concentrating their efforts on a cultured, white audience. That same year a review of public broadcasting stations' top three job categories (officials, managers, and professionals) showed that 108 of the 184 public radio licensees and 52 of the 160 public television licensees had no minority staff at these levels.

In the early 1990s the highest-ranking African Americans in public television were Jennifer Lawson, Donald L. Marbury, and George L. Miles, Jr. Lawson was responsible for securing and promoting the programs the Public Broadcasting Service (PBS) provides to its member stations. Marbury was charged with managing the $45 million television program fund of the Corporation for Public Broadcasting, which provides funding support for major series in public television, such as *Frontline*. Miles served as executive vice president and chief operating officer of WNET-TV in New York.

The most visible African American journalist on public television has been *MacNeil Lehrer News Hour* correspondent Charlayne Hunter-Gault, a former *New York Times* reporter noted for her in-depth reporting. Other black journalists with the show include Washington correspondent Kwame Holman and producer Jackie Farmer. PBS's most acclaimed piece of African American journalism was *Eyes on the Prize,* a history of the civil rights movement produced by Henry Hampton, which aired in 1987, with a sequel in 1990. Its most controversial was a one-hour film on black homosexual men, *Tongues Untied,* by filmmaker Marlon Riggs in 1991.

In 1980 Howard University launched WHMM-TV, becoming the first licensee of a public television station on a black campus and the only black-owned public television station in the nation. On August 31, 1991, San Francisco's Minority Television Project went on the air with KMTP0-TV, which became the nation's second black-owned public television station. One of the principals was Adam Clayton Powell III, son of the late Harlem congressman.

Public Radio

Before 1967 there were only two black educational outlets in the country; by 1990 there were 40 black public radio stations. Many of them were community radio stations, owned and operated by nonprofit foundations, controlled by a local board of directors, and funded by listener donations. Others were on college campuses. One of the most successful was WPFW-FM, launched in 1977 by the Pacifica Foundation.

Stations such as WCLK-FM at Clark College in Atlanta, WBVA-FM in Harrodsburg, Kentucky, and WVAS-FM at Alabama State University in Montgomery tailored news and public affairs programming to their local African American audiences. Students majoring in the field used WVAS as a broadcast journalism lab. On National Public Radio, journalists Phyllis Crockett, Vertamae Grosvenor, Cheryl Duvall, and Brenda Wilson have won awards for reports on South Africa and issues involving African Americans.

Cable Television

The 1980s saw the explosion of cable television and the decline of the television networks. Black Entertainment Television, founded by former congressional aide Robert L. Johnson, made its debut in 1980 and established a news division by the end of the decade. That division produced a weekly news show, *BET News,* and *Lead Story,* a talk show featuring black **pundits.**

The biggest development in cable journalism, however, was the spectacular growth of Ted Turner's Cable News Network (CNN), which went on line in June 1980. By the 1991 Persian Gulf war, CNN had established itself as the station to watch in a crisis. Transmitted across the globe, it became a medium for world leaders to communicate among one another.

Veteran journalist Bernard Shaw, principal Washington anchor, was one of three CNN reporters who captivated the world with continuous coverage of the first night of bombing on Baghdad on January 16, 1991. Other African Americans at CNN include Jay Suber, vice president and executive producer, news features, CNN Newsroom; Graylian Young, Southeast bureau chief; CNN anchors Andrea Arceneaux, Leon Harris, and Joe Oliver; Cassandra Henderson, anchor for CNN Newsroom; Lyn Vaughn and Gordon Graham, Headline News anchors; sports anchor Fred Hickman; and correspondent Norma Quarles.

Book Publishers

Religious Publishers

Various black churches established religious publishing enterprises in order to publish and record **denominational** history and provide religious instruction. Some black religious publishers also published books on **secular** subjects, which were generally related to celebrating some aspect of black culture or documenting black history.

Prior to the Civil War, two black religious publishing enterprises existed. The African Methodist Episcopal Church organized the AME Book Concern in Philadelphia in 1817 and became the first black-owned book publishing enterprise in the United States. The AME Book Concern published a host of classic religious and secular books until its operations were suspended in 1952 by the General Conference of the AME Church.

In 1841 the African Methodist Episcopal Zion Church formed the AME Zion Book Concern in New York City. This firm, which only published religious works, was moved to its present location in Charlotte, North Carolina, in 1894, where it continues to be an active book publisher.

In Jackson, Tennessee, the Colored Methodist Episcopal Church, presently known as the Christian Methodist Episcopal Church, started the CME Publishing House in 1870. The CME Publishing House, which only publishes books on religious subjects, is currently located in Memphis.

Another book publishing enterprise owned by black Methodists is the AME Sunday School Union and Publishing House, which was established in Bloomington, Illinois, in 1882; AME moved to Nashville, Tennessee, in 1886. Publishing secular and religious books, this enterprise remains the oldest publishing unit owned by the African Methodist Episcopal Church.

One of the most successful black religious publishers founded during the nineteenth century was the National Baptist Publishing Board. Under the leadership of Richard Henry Boyd and the sponsorship of the National Baptist Convention, the National Baptist Publishing Board was organized in Nashville in 1896. By 1913 this well-managed firm had become one of the largest black-owned businesses in the United States.

In 1915, however, a dispute arose between the National Baptist Convention and Boyd over the ownership of the National Baptist Publishing Board. In a court suit, the Tennessee Supreme Court decided in favor of Boyd. Today the National Publishing Board, owned by the Boyd family, is a thriving religious publishing enterprise.

In 1907 the Church of God in Christ established the Church of God in Christ Publishing House in Memphis. Restricting its publications to religious books and pamphlets, this publisher continues today to meet the ever-expanding needs for religious literature for one of the fastest growing black denominations in the United States.

Faced with the loss of the National Baptist Publishing Board, the National Baptist Convention established in 1916 the Sunday School Publishing Board in Nashville. Over the years, this firm has developed into one of the largest black-owned publishing enterprises in the United States, publishing religious and secular books and pamphlets.

Like the Sunday School Publishing Board, Muhammad's Temple No. 2 Publications Department, founded in 1956 by the Nation of Islam, published religious as well as secular books. Between 1956 and 1974 this firm issued several books; since 1974, however, the Publications Department has been inactive.

Institutional Publishers

Colleges and Universities

Hampton Institute became the first black educational institution to publish books when the Hampton Institute Press was established in 1871. An active publisher until 1940, the Hampton Institute Press published travel books, poetry, textbooks, songbooks, and conference proceedings. Hampton also published *The Southern Workman,* one of the leading national African American periodicals published between 1871 and 1939, the year of its demise.

In 1896 the Atlanta University Press entered the book publishing market with the release of the "Atlanta University Publication Series," **monographs** reporting on studies conducted by the university's sociology department under the direction of W.E.B. Du Bois. These works represented some of the earliest studies in urban sociology conducted in the South. The Atlanta University Press remained in operation until 1936.

The first book released by the Tuskegee Institute Press was *Industrial Work of Tuskegee Graduates and Former Students During the Year 1910,* compiled by Monroe N. Work. With the publication of this book and other works by the press, Tuskegee founder Booker T. Washington publicized the success of Tuskegee's program to white **philanthropists** in the North. The Tuskegee Institute Press, which was active until 1958, published several other important works, including John Kenny's *The Negroes in Med-*

icine (1912) and Jessie Parkhurst Guzman's *Lynching by States, 1882-1958* (1958).

In 1910 another book publishing enterprise, the Negro Yearbook Publishing Company, was launched on the campus of Tuskegee Institute. This firm—consisting of a partnership among white sociologist Robert E. Park, Washington's secretary Emmett J. Scott, and sociology professor Monroe N. Work—published the first edition of *The Negro Yearbook* in 1912. The *Yearbook* was highly regarded as the best and most thorough collection of statistics and facts on blacks worldwide. However, the Negro Yearbook Publishing Company fell into financial trouble in 1929 and was taken over by Tuskegee Institute, which financed its operation until 1952. Between 1912 and 1952 *The Negro Yearbook* remained a classic model for most general reference works on blacks.

John W. Work's *The Negro and His Song* (1915) was the first book issued under the Fisk University Press imprint. During the 1930s and 1940s, when Charles Spurgeon Johnson chaired the university's department of sociology, several important studies were issued by the Fisk University Press. These included *The Free Negro Family* by E. Franklin Frazier (1932); *The Economic Status of the Negro* by Charles Spurgeon Johnson (1933), and *People versus Property* by Herman Long and Charles Spurgeon Johnson (1947). The last publication released by the Fisk University Press was *Build a Future: Addresses Marking the Inauguration of Charles Spurgeon Johnson* (1949).

Although the board of trustees of Howard University approved the establishment of a university press on February 17, 1919, it was not organized until 1974. Nonetheless, between 1919 and 1974 several books bearing the "Howard University Press" imprint were published. On April 8, 1974, the Howard University Press was officially organized as a separate unit within the university with a staff of 12 professionals experienced in book publishing. The Howard University Press's initial list of 13 books included such titles as *A Poetic Equation: Conversations between Nikki Giovanni and Margaret Walker* (1974) and *Saw the House in Half, a Novel* by Oliver Jackman (1974). The Howard University Press continues to flourish as one of the most distinguished university presses in the country.

Cultural and Professional Organizations and Institutions

Black cultural and professional organizations have also developed book publishing programs. The books published by these organizations document many areas of black history and many aspects of African American culture.

Founded in 1897 by black scholar, clergyman, and missionary Alexander Crummell, the American Negro Academy quickly organized a publishing program that embraced book publishing. The Academy, whose membership included many of the foremost black thinkers of the day, released 21 separate pamphlets and monographs before folding in 1928.

The Association for the Study of Negro Life and History (now the Association for the Study of Afro-American History and Literature) began its book publishing program in 1918. By 1940 the association had published 28 books. After that year, the Association's publishing program declined until 1950, when its founder, Carter G.

Woodson, died and provided in his will for the transfer of the Associated Publishers, Inc. to the Association.

The Associates of Negro Folk Education, organized in Washington, D.C., by Howard University philosophy professor Alain Locke with a grant from the American Adult Education Association, published a series of seven books, known as the "Bronze Booklets," from 1935 to 1940. Written by black scholars on various aspects of black American life and edited by Locke, some of these titles included *A World View of Race* by Ralph J. Bunche (1936), *The Negro and Economic Reconstruction* by T. Arnold Hill (1937), and *Negro Poetry and Drama* by Sterling Brown (1937).

Civil Rights, Social Welfare, and Political Organizations

In 1913, five years after its founding, the NAACP launched its publishing program with three books: Julia L. Henderson's *A Child's Story of Dunbar* (1919), Maude Cuney Hare's *Norris Wright Cuney* (1913), and Mary White Ovington's *Hazel* (1913). In 1914 George Williamson Crawford's *Prince Hall and His Followers* appeared and in 1919 *Thirty Years of Lynching in the United States, 1889-1918* was released. After 1919 few books were published by the NAACP. Instead, the organization limited its publishing to *Crisis* magazine, pamphlets, and its annual reports.

In contrast, the National Urban League has been a very active book publisher. The League first entered into book publishing in 1927 with *Ebony and Topaz,* an anthology of **Harlem Renaissance** writers, poets, and artists edited by Charles Spurgeon Johnson.

Through the years numerous studies on the plight of black Americans have been published by the Urban League, including *Negro Membership in Labor Unions* (1930), *Race, Fear and Housing in a Typical American Community* (1946), and *Power of the Ballot: A Handbook for Black Political Participation* (1973). In addition to these studies, the organization began publishing the annual *The State of Black America* in 1976.

Although the publishing program of the Universal Negro Improvement Association and African Communities League focused on the publication its newspaper, *The Negro World,* this political organization also published books. Two volumes of *The Philosophy and Opinions of Marcus Garvey,* compiled and edited by Amy Jacques-Garvey, were published under the imprint of the Press of the Universal Negro Improvement Association.

Commercial Publishers

Until the 1960s most black commercial businesses engaged in book publishing were short-lived. However, in 1967 Haki Madhubuti founded Third World Press in Chicago. Third World Press is now the oldest continually operating black commercial book publisher in the United States.

Over the years, black publishers have discovered that a sizable black readership exists; consequently, since 1970 several major black publishers have emerged. In 1978 Black Classic Press was founded by librarian Paul Coates to publish works by and about people of African descent. In 1978 Dempsey Travis founded Urban Research Press. Open Hand Publishing Inc. was founded in 1981 by Anna Johnson.

In 1983 Kassahun Checole founded Africa World Press to publish material on the economic, political, and social development of Africa. Checole, a former African studies instructor at Rutgers University, found it difficult to obtain books needed for his courses. Now African World Press publishes nearly 60 titles a year and its sister company, Red Sea Press, has become one of the largest distributors of material by and about Africans.

Just Us Books, Inc., founded by writer Wade Hudson and graphic artist Cheryl Willis Hudson, publishes books and educational material for children that focus on the African American experience. The idea to start the children's book publisher first came to Hudson in 1976, when she was unable to find black images to decorate her daughter's nursery. Just Us Books published its first book in 1988—an alphabet book featuring African American children.

22
Music

Popular, Jazz, and Classical

"To be a great musician, you've got to be open to what's new, what's happening at the moment. You have to be able to absorb it if you're going to continue to grow and communicate."—Miles Davis

"Jazz and freedom go hand in hand."—Thelonius Monk

Popular Music

Since the turn of the twentieth century, black music—whether gospel, rhythm and blues, rock and roll, soul, funk, or rap—has shaped American popular music. More recently, its impact can be heard in the emergence of world music coming out of Africa, South America, and the Caribbean Islands. From the church to the concert stage, thousands of gifted African American singers and musicians have given the United States and the world a gift of unbounding spirit.

Gospel: The Root of Popular Music

The foundation of twentieth-century black popular music is rooted in the sounds of several folk styles. These include black minstrel and vaudeville tunes, blues, and ragtime. However, black religious music has played one of the most crucial roles in the evolution of black popular music.

Slaves used religious songs to express their present misery and their hope for the future. In this fashion, "Go Down Moses," "Oh Freedom," "God's Gonna Cut You Down," and many other spirituals have become part of the vast oral tradition created by the black musical artist. After the Civil War, the Fisk Jubilee Singers extended the realm of the Negro spiritual to the international arena by going on a tour of Europe with "Negro" music as the basis of their **repertoire.**

Closely tied to slave spirituals was gospel music, which came to dominate the black religious experience in America. By the end of the 1800s gospel music had reached great popularity as black religious songwriters began to publish their own compositions. One of the earliest and most influential of these writers was Charles Albert Tindley, a Maryland-born Methodist preacher. His song "I'll Overcome Someday" resurfaced more than a half century later as "We Shall Overcome," the anthem of the 1960s civil rights movement. Tindley's 1905 composition "Stand by Me" also became a major hit—for singer Ben E. King and the Drifters—during the 1960s.

The Father of Gospel Music

Tindley's music influenced Thomas A. Dorsey, whose talents as a religious songwriter, accompanist, and choir director earned him the title "the father of gospel music." Before dedicating his life to the Baptist church, Dorsey spent his youth as a

WORDS TO KNOW

arias: melodies in an opera, oratorio, or cantata created especially for a solo voice

avant-garde: new and nontraditional

conglomerate: a large corporation that owns several smaller businesses in a number of different industries

connoisseurs: those who take keen enjoyment in their field of expertise

disenfranchised: the poor or disadvantaged

militancy: aggressiveness; a willingness to fight for a cause

misogyny: hatred of women

nationalist: in black studies, one who believes in the creation of black power through a politically and economically strong black nation

psychedelic: causing intense stimulation of the mind

repertoire: songs or pieces within a musician's or group of musicians' typical performance program

syncopated: shifted in beat from what is regularly accented to what is regularly unaccented

tenure: a permanent right to a position, as in teaching

timpanist: a player of kettledrums (timpani)

virtuoso: someone with extraordinary skill in a given field

Thomas A. Dorsey with his group, the Wandering Syncopators Orchestra, 1923

roving blues pianist, performing under the name Georgia Tom. Like other bluesmen/preachers such as Reverend Gary Davis, Blind Willie McTell, and Gatemouth Moore, Dorsey performed both secular and religious music. In 1928, for example, he cowrote the blues hit "Tight Like That" with guitarist Hudson "Tampa Red" Whitaker and composed his first gospel song, "If You See My Savior Tell Him You Saw Me."

Four years later Dorsey abandoned his career as a blues and jazz pianist to devote himself to a form of religious music that historian Michael W. Harris describes as

gospel-blues style, blending black religious and popular music into a unique and passionate form of gospel. During the Great Depression, Dorsey's new style of gospel served as a release from the poverty and gloom experienced in the black community.

In 1930 the performance of two of Dorsey's songs at the National Baptist Convention created a wave of enthusiasm for gospel across the nation. In the following year, Dorsey organized the world's first gospel choir. In 1932 he began a 40-year career as choir director at Chicago's Pilgrim Baptist Church. During his stay at Pilgrim

W. C. Handy

Baptist, he launched the golden age of gospel music, training and accompanying singers from Sallie Martin to Mahalia Jackson.

Gospel and the Recording Industry

The distribution of records helped break down the musical isolation imposed upon blacks since slavery and allowed them to reach audiences outside their own communities. Recorded by the Victor label in 1902, the Jubilee and camp meeting shouts of the Dwinddie Colored Quartet appeared as one of the first black recordings. In the 1920s black religious music became popular with the race record (a title designating the segregated sale of African American recordings).

By 1924 Paramount Records sponsored its own Jubilee singers, and within three years Columbia Records began to send engineers into the field to record the richly complex harmonies of gospel quartets. Also popular were recorded sermons backed by occasional musical instruments, and evangelistic guitars, known commonly as "jack legs," which brought street singing gospel blues to a wider audience.

After a decline in recordings by evangelists during the 1930s and early 1940s, gospel music experienced an immense rise in popularity as hundreds of independent recording labels appeared after World War II. During the 1940s numerous gospel quartets went on the road as full-time professionals, while thousands more sought work on weekends. Dressed in flowing robes and fashionably designed dress suits, quartets incorporated dance routines and expressive shouts into their performances. Throughout the postwar period, such male gospel quartets as the Five Blind Boys from Mississippi, the Mighty Clouds of Joy from Los Angeles, and the Sensational Nightingales from Memphis sang a capella (without instruments) on numerous recordings.

The Rise of Rhythm and Blues

As black veterans returned home from World War II, they found not only a new gospel sound, but an exciting blues style, called jump blues, being played by small combos. With its roots in boogie woogie and the blues-swing arrangements of Count Basie, Cab Calloway, Louis Jordan, and others, this new blues style acquired an enormous following in black urban areas across the country. Unlike the swing-era big bands, jump blues groups featured fewer horns and a heavy rhythmic approach marked by a

Louis Jordan and the Tympany Five, 1946

walking boogie bass line, honking saxophone solos, and a two-four drum pattern. Among the greatest masters of postwar jump blues were guitarist T-Bone Walker, saxophonist Eddie "Cleanhead" Vincent, and blues shouter Big Joe Turner.

Soon many jump blues ensembles began to feature singers versed in a smooth, gospel-influenced vocal style. In 1949 the popularity of this style led *Billboard Magazine* to change its black pop chart title to rhythm and blues, thus coining the name of this new music. Just as blues and religious spirituals and hymns formed gospel, rhythm

and blues drew upon gospel, electric urban blues, and swing jazz to create a vibrantly modern sound appealing to the younger generation of postwar blacks. Some of the early recordings illustrating the gospel influence on rhythm and blues were Cecil Grant's 1945 hit "I Wonder," Roy Brown's 1947 classic "Good Rocking Tonight," and Wynonie Harris's 1949 disc "All She Wants to Do Is Rock."

With the increased number of rhythm and blues recordings, a handful of black radio disc jockeys became locally famous as the first promoters and salesmen of this music.

Bessie Smith, "Empress of the Blues"

Bringing their colorful street language to the airwaves, pioneer black DJs such as Al Benson and Vernon Winslow not only helped to popularize R&B, but also set the trend for modern pop radio.

R&B and the Black Church

In the early 1950s numerous gospel quartets and street corner singing groups set out to establish careers in the black popular music scene. Influenced by gospel music and such mainstream groups as the Inkspots, vocal groups appeared performing complex harmonies in a capella style. Urban street corners became training grounds for thousands of hopeful African American artists. This music, known as doo-wop, first arrived

on the scene with the formation of the Ravens in 1945.

Shortly after there came a great string of doo-wop "bird groups" including the Orioles who, in 1953, scored a nationwide hit with "Crying in the Chapel"—a song which, for the first time in black popular music, walked an almost undistinguishable line between gospel and mainstream pop music. In the same year Billy Ward formed the Dominoes, featuring lead singer Clyde McPhatter.

In the wake of the success of these vocal groups, numerous gospel singers left the church to become pop music stars. In 1952, for example, the Royal Sons became the Five Royales, the Gospel Starlighters (with James Brown), and finally the Blue Flames. Five years later a young gospel singer

Sam Cooke

495

Billie Holiday, still a powerful force in music decades after her untimely death

named Sam Cooke landed a number-one pop hit with "You Send Me," which achieved popularity among both black and white audiences.

The strong relationship between gospel and rhythm and blues was evident in the music of more hard-edged R&B groups, including Hank Ballard and the Midnighters. Maintaining a driving blues-based sound, Ballard's music featured gospel harmonies and everyday themes, as evidenced in his 1954 hit "Work with Me Annie." However, the capstone of gospel R&B appeared with Georgia-born pianist and singer Ray Charles, who in 1954 hit the charts with "I Got a Woman," which was based upon the gospel song "My Jesus Is All the World to Me." Charles's 1958 recording "What I'd Say" is famed for its call-and-response pattern that directly resembled the music sung in Holiness churches.

Rock and Roll

The rise of white rock and roll around 1955 opened the floodgates for thousands of black R&B artists longing for a nationwide audience. Applied to black R&B and its white equivalents during the mid-1950s, the term rock and roll (which actually came from the Mississippi Delta and electric blues cultures) was used in order to attract a mass multiracial audience.

Chuck Berry

Frutti." Before entering a Seventh Day Adventist seminary in 1959, Little Richard produced a string of hits, including "Long Tall Sally," "Rip It Up," "The Girl Can't Help It," and "Good Golly Miss Molly."

In 1955, as Fats Domino's New Orleans style R&B tunes climbed the charts, a young guitarist from St. Louis named Chuck Berry achieved nationwide fame with a country-influenced song entitled "Maybelline," which reached number five on the charts. Backed by bluesman Muddy Waters's rhythm section, "Maybelline" offered a unique form of R&B combining white hillbilly, or Rockabilly, with jump blues. Berry revolutionized R&B by featuring the guitar as a lead, rather than a rhythm instrument. Modeled after his blues-guitar mentor T-Bone Walker, Berry's double string guitar bends and **syncopated** up-stroke rhythm created a driving backdrop for his colorfully poetic tales of teenage life. A highly creative musician, Berry incorporated the sounds of urban blues, country, calypso, Latin, and even Hawaiian music into his unique brand of R&B. His classic "Johnny B. Goode," recorded in 1958, became a standard in almost every rock and roll band's repertoire, including that of rock guitar hero Jimi Hendrix.

Blacks and Country Music

Berry was not the only African American to take an interest in country music. Ray Charles's crossover into country music in the early 1960s caused controversy in many circles. In 1959 Charles recorded "I'm Moving On," a country tune by Hank Snow. Despite opposition, Charles went on to record a fine collection of songs in 1962 titled *Modern Sounds in Country Music.*

Thus, the majority of R&B performers never made the distinction between rhythm and blues and rock and roll. One R&B artist who made a particularly successful transition to rock and roll was New Orleans-born pianist Antoine "Fats" Domino. Although he had produced a great amount of strong R&B material before his career in rock and roll, Domino did not hit the charts until 1955 with "Ain't That A Shame," followed by the classics "Blueberry Hill," "I'm Walkin," and "Whole Lotta Loving."

Another R&B pianist/singer to enter the rock and roll field was Little Richard Penniman, a former gospel singer whose career in pop music began in 1956 with the hit "Tutti

Filled with soulful ballads and backed by colorful string sections, the session produced two classic numbers, "You Don't Know Me" and "I Can't Stop Loving You." Its popularity spawned a 1963 sequel, *Modern Sounds in Country Music Volume 2,* containing several more hits, including Hank Williams's "Your Cheating Heart" and "Take These Chains from My Heart." Unlike other mainstream black country artists, Charles's renditions rarely strayed from his unique gospel-blues sound.

Before Charles crossed over to country there had been many African American country artists. A prime example was Deford Bailey, a disabled harmonica player who became a regularly featured performer on the Grand Ole Opry from 1925 to 1941. However, it was not until Charley Pride arrived on the country music scene in 1965 with his RCA recordings "Snakes Crawl at Night" and "Atlantic Coastal Line" that a black artist emerged as a superstar in the country tradition.

Pride's songs were so steeped in the country tradition that many radio listeners were astounded when they found out his racial identity. With the arrival of Pride, there appeared other black country artists, including Linda Martel from South Carolina, O. B. McClinton from Mississippi, and Oklahoma-born Big Al Downing and Stoney Edwards. The most noted of these artists, Edwards recorded two nationwide hits in 1968, Jesse Winchester's "You're on My Mind" and Leonard Cohen's "Bird on a Wire."

Soul: The Mirror of a Decade

The most dominant form of black popular music of the 1960s, however, emerged

Aretha Franklin

under the powerful gospel-influenced rhythm and blues style known as soul. This new music crossed over by 1965 or 1966; despite traces of its influence throughout modern culture, however, it had all but faded by the early 1970s. Because it paralleled the 1960s civil rights and black power movements, soul embodied a sense of racial pride and independence. Such themes are evident in the soul music of Curtis Mayfield, whose "People Get Ready" (1965), "We're a Winner" (1965), and "Choice of Color" (1969) represented messages of racial advancement and social change.

Soul music was also strongly linked to the music of the black church. In fact, during the 1960s a distinct pattern emerged among African American artists, who often

James Brown

established careers in gospel music before becoming R&B and soul artists. Among those who followed this pattern were soul singers Solomon Burke, Wilson Pickett, and Otis Redding.

One could say that soul intensified the gospel influence in popular black music. Soul artists from Joe Tex to Aretha Franklin, the "Lady of Soul," cultivated and refined a passionate form of singing filled with gospel-influenced shouts and screams. With the addition of the electric bass, which replaced the acoustic bass featured on most of the R&B music of the 1940s and 1950s, these singers commanded a modern pulsing rhythm that inspired them to reshape the sound of black music.

In 1965 Wilson Pickett released "Midnight Hour" and Otis Redding hit the charts with the ballad "I've Been Loving You Too Long." That same year a dynamic veteran of the gospel and R&B circuit named James Brown climbed the charts with a powerful soul number entitled "Out of Sight."

A self-created legend, Brown was a genius of soul music. As "Soul Brother No. 1," he achieved commercial success with his legendary 1963 LP *Live at the Apollo,* a record many critics believe best captures his explosive onstage energy. Throughout the 1960s Brown astounded audiences with his ability to lead a full horn and rhythm section through unrehearsed changes in the musical form by a sudden gesture or a quick vocal command. Later in the decade Brown and his powerful rhythm section, the Famous Flames, produced a number of classic soul numbers such as "Papa's Got a Brand New Bag," "Cold Sweat," and "I'm Black and I'm Proud." The "James Brown Sound" not only had a profound impact on the development of funk and jazz fusion, but it also helped shape the sound of African popular music.

Motown: The Capital of Northern Soul

While soul music gained a mass following in the black community during the 1960s, a black-owned and family-run Detroit record company emerged as one of the largest and most successful African American business enterprises in America. Named after Detroit's own nickname, the Motown Record Corporation was the brainchild of Berry Gordy, an entrepreneur, songwriter, and modern jazz enthusiast.

With its headquarters located in a modest two-story home, the company proudly displayed a sign on its exterior reading Hitsville USA. Taking advantage of the

The Supremes

wide range of local talent, Gordy employed Detroit-based contract teams, writers, producers, and engineers. Motown's studio became a great laboratory for technological innovations, advancing the use of echo, multitracking, and overdubbing. In the studio, Gordy employed the city's finest jazz and classical musicians to accompany the young singers signed to the company.

Unlike the soul music emerging in studios like Stax Records in Memphis and Muscle Shoals Sounds in Alabama, Motown's music was also marketed to the white middle class. Gordy called his music "The Sound of Young America" and sought to produce glamorous and well-groomed acts. "Blues and R&B always had a funky look to it back in those days," explained Motown producer Mickey Stevenson. "We felt that we should have a look that the mothers and fathers would want their children to follow."

Thus, Motown set out to produce a sound that it considered to be more refined and less "off-key" than the music played by mainstream soul and blues artists. In its early years of operation, Motown retained an R&B influence as evidenced in songs like the Marvellettes' "Please Mister Post-

QUINCY JONES

Winner of 20 Grammy Awards, Quincy Jones remains one of the most successful black musician/producers in pop music. Among his most important projects was the production of the 1985 Number 1 single "We Are the World," written by Michael Jackson and Lionel Richie and sung by the largest special gathering of musical celebrities in history.

man" (1961), Mary Wells's "You Beat Me to the Punch" (1962), and Marvin Gaye's "Pride and Joy" (1963).

One of the main forces responsible for the unique "Motown sound" was the production team of Brian Holland, Eddie Holland, and Lamont Dozier, or H-D-H, as they came to be known. Utilizing the recording techniques of Phil Spector's "wall of sound," the H-D-H team brought fame to many of Motown's "girl-groups," including Martha and the Vandellas and the Supremes, featuring Diana Ross.

Around 1966 H-D-H began to use more complex string arrangements based upon minor chord structures. This gave rise to what has been referred to as their "classical period." As a result, many Motown songs reflected the darker side of lost love and the conditions of ghetto life. This mood was captured in such Four Tops songs as "Reach Out I'll Be There," "Bernadette," and "Seven Rooms of Gloom."

After the Holland-Dozier-Holland team left Motown in 1968, the company, faced with numerous money and artistic problems, began to decline. A year later Gordy signed the Jackson 5, the last major act to join the label before its demise. The Jacksons landed 13 consecutive hit singles, including "ABC" and "I'll Be There." In 1971 Gordy moved the Motown Record Corporation to Los Angeles, where the company directed its efforts toward filmmaking. Through the late 1970s and early 1980s Motown continued to sign such acts as the Commodores, Lionel Richie, and DeBarge. But in 1984 Gordy entered into a distribution agreement with MCA records and eventually sold Motown to an entertainment **conglomerate.**

Funk

With the retreat of Motown in the 1970s, a new African American music style appeared that met the demands for a harder-edged dance music. The origins of what became funk can be traced to several sources: the music of James Brown, the rhythm patterns of New Orleans drummer Ziggy Modeliste, and the slapping electric bass style of Sly and the Family Stone member Larry Graham. Funk capitalized on the modern guitar styles of Jimi Hendrix and Johnny "Guitar" Watson. It also brought the synthesizer to the forefront of pop music, which gave funk a textual and rhythmic quality unlike the music played by the soul bands of the 1960s.

By the 1970s a number of groups played in the funk style, including soul veterans Curtis Mayfield and the Isley Brothers, and Maurice White's Earth, Wind, and Fire. Under George "Dr. Funkenstein" Clinton, there appeared a series of blended bands bearing the titles Parliment, Funkadelic,

Jimi Hendrix

Bootsy's Rubber Band, the Horny Horns, and the Brides of Funkenstein, to name a few. Blending **psychedelic** guitar lines, complex chord work, and vocal distortion, Parliment-Funkadelic created a gritty funk style that sought to counter the sounds of the 1970s disco craze.

Other bands to join the funk scene were Kool and the Gang, the Ohio Players, and the Commodores. Although more refined in style than Parliment-Funkadelic, these groups still kept a soul-influenced sound in an era when the commercial sounds of disco dominated the popular music scene.

Rap: A Voice from the Streets

While funk sold millions of records and received extensive radio airplay in the mid-1970s, rap music was beginning to emerge within a small circle of New York artists and entertainers. In neighborhoods in Upper Manhattan and the South Bronx, disc jockeys at private parties discovered how to use "little raps" between songs to keep dancers on their feet. From behind the microphone, DJs created a call and response pattern with the audience. "Soon a division of labor emerged," explained Jefferson Morley, "and DJs concentrated on perfecting the techniques of manipulating the turntables, while masters of ceremonies (MCs or rappers) focused on rapping in rhymes." Through the use of a special stylus, rappers moved records back and forth on the turntable in order to create a unique rhythmic sound, known within the rap culture as needle rocking.

Long before the modern rap, or hip-hop, culture appeared, however, there were African American artists who performed in a rap-type style. In 1929, for instance, New York singer-comedian Pigmeat Markham gave performances suggestive of an early rap-style.

Rap music is also rooted in the talking jazz style of a group of ex-convicts called the Last Poets. During the 1960s this group of black intellectuals rapped in complex rhythms over music played by jazz accompanists. Last Poet member Jalal Uridin, recording under the name Lightning Rod, released an album titled *Hustler's Convention*. Backed by the funk band Kool and the Gang, Uridin's recording became very influential to the early New York rappers.

Among one of the first New York rap

artists of the early 1970s was Jamaican-born Clive Campbell, aka Cool Herc. As a street DJ, Herc developed the art of sampling: the method of playing a section of a recording over and over in order to create a unique dance mix. Others to join the New York scene were black **nationalist** DJ Africa Bambaataa, from the southeast Bronx, and Joseph Saddler, known as Grandmaster Flash, from the central Bronx. Flash formed the group Grandmaster Flash and The Three MCs (Cowboy, Kid Creole, and Melle Mel). Later he added Kurtis Blow and Duke Bootee, who founded the Furious Five.

However, rap music did not reach a broad audience until 1980 when the Sugar Hill Gang's song "Rapper's Delight" received widespread radio play. As rap groups assembled during the decade, they began to use their art to describe the harsh realities of inner city life. Unlike early rap music, which was generally upbeat and exuberant in tone, the rap style of the 1980s displayed a strong racial and political awareness. Toward the end of the decade, rap came to express an increasing sense of racial **militancy.**

Inspired by the Nation of Islam and the teachings of Malcolm X, such rap groups as Public Enemy turned their music into a voice supporting black power. Public Enemy's second LP, *It Takes A Nation of Millions to Hold Us Back,* sold over one million copies. Their song "Fight the Power" appeared in director Spike Lee's film *Do the Right Thing.* The group's third album, *Fear of a Black Planet,* was released in 1990. While it is a statement against "western cultural supremacy," explained group member Chuck D, it is also "about the coming together of all races" in a "racial rebirth."

Queen Latifah

Women have also played a role in the shaping of rap music. Rap artists such as Queen Latifah and the group Salt-N-Pepa represent a growing number of female rappers who speak for the advancement of black women in American society. Queen Latifah has emerged as a critic of male dominance in the music industry and sexist images of women presented by some male rap artists.

In addition to racial protest, rap has been associated with such topics as **misogyny,** sex, and youth culture. In other instances, rap seeks to educate young listeners about the dangers of inner-city life. But no matter what style, rap is the voice of many young African Americans. Like the music of earlier black artists, rap is filled with energy, creativity, and descriptions of the human experience. "Rap is no fad," contends Quincy Jones, "and it's not just a new kind of music. It's a whole new subculture that's been invented by the **disenfranchised.**"

Blues and Jazz

In less than a century, jazz music has risen from obscurity to become the most original and universal form of musical expression of our times. Jazz has a long and rich ancestry. Its roots go back to the arrival of the first Africans on American soil and the encounter between native African and European musical traditions.

Ragtime and Blues

By the late nineteenth century a dance music called ragtime became very popular. Its lively melodies and heavily syncopated rhythms had a distinctly African American flavor. Ragtime's greatest artist was Scott Joplin (1868-1917); all but forgotten by the time of his death, Joplin's music was redis-covered during the 1970s.

During ragtime's brief, original heyday, a form of black American folk music called the blues merged into a 12-bar pattern that made it adaptable to popular songwriting. The blues has a unique harmonic quality derived from a "flattening" of the third and seventh notes of the tempered scale and, while seemingly simple, lends itself to end-less variation. The blues had an impact on jazz and later influenced such styles as rock and soul music, both of which would be unthinkable without the blues element.

New Orleans Jazz

Jazz was born when the styles of ragtime (primarily instrumental) and blues (at first

Scott Joplin

primarily vocal) came together. Though this process was taking place in many parts of America, it was in New Orleans that the basic language of jazz was first spoken. This was partly due to the rich musical tradition of this port city; it was also due to the fact that New Orleans society, while certainly not free from racist elements, was more open to racial intermixing than other large American cities of the time. Thus, there was much contact between musicians of varied ethnic backgrounds.

Many histories of jazz mistakenly stress the importance of the New Orleans red light district (called Storyville). Although early jazz was performed in Storyville, there were many other outlets for music-making. These included dances, parades, carnivals, and

Louis Armstrong in Duesseldorf, Germany, 1956

funerals. In traditional New Orleans funerals, a band accompanied the casket with mournful strains from church to cemetery. On the way back to town, the band led the march with the lively, peppy music sounds of ragtime and early jazz music.

Musicians from New Orleans began to tour the United States around 1907 and were influential wherever they went. However, their style of improvisation, in which each instrument in the band had its own specific role, was not so easily absorbed. (Improvisation is a much misunderstood concept. It does not mean inventing music on the spot, without guidelines. It does mean adding one's own personal ideas to a common musical text, and taking liberties that fit within a shared framework.) It is another myth of jazz history that most of these early jazz players were a special breed of self-taught "naturals." In fact, almost all of them had good basic musical training, and many could read music well.

Early Recordings and Improvisation

Jazz and the phonograph surfaced at almost the same time. This was important; without records it is unlikely that jazz would have spread as quickly as it did. By studying recorded performances, musicians anywhere could learn at least the basics of jazz, a spontaneous music in which improvisation played a considerable role.

Strangely enough, the first New Orleans jazz to be recorded was performed by a white group, the Original Dixieland Jazz Band, in 1917. Although black musicians had already made records by that time, they were not in a jazz style; it took another five years before the best black New Orleans players followed suit. In the meanwhile, some of them had already begun playing overseas. One such musician was the great clarinetist and soprano saxophonist Sidney Bechet (1897-1959), who has been called the first great jazz soloist. But it was another New Orleanian, Louis Armstrong (1901-1971), who would have the biggest impact on the future of jazz.

Armstrong was brought to Chicago (by then the center of jazz activity) in 1922 by mentor and fellow trumpeter Joe "King" Oliver (1885-1938). Two years later, after making his first recordings in Chicago, Armstrong came to New York to join the band of Fletcher Henderson (1897-1952). This was the first musically significant big band in jazz.

Armstrong's arrival was a revelation to the Henderson band. His first solos for the band's records stand out like diamonds in a tin setting. What he brought to jazz was, first of all, his superior sense of rhythm that made other players sound stiff and clumsy in comparison. Armstrong discovered the rhythmic element called "swing" that sets jazz apart from other musical styles. In addition, his sound on the trumpet was the

Jazz greats Ella Fitzgerald, Oscar Peterson (piano), Roy Eldridge (trumpet), and Max Roach (drums), 1952

biggest and most musically appealing yet heard, and he had exceptional range and powers of execution. Further, his gifts of invention were so great that he is often considered the first soloist who made jazz a medium for personal expression.

One of the first Henderson colleagues to "get the message" was tenor saxophonist Coleman Hawkins (1904-1969), who soon created the first influential jazz style on his instrument. Also greatly affected was the band's chief arranger, Don Redman (1900-1964), who was the first to translate Armstrong's discoveries to big-band arranging. Many other disciples emerged, especially after Armstrong, now back in Chicago, began to make records with his own studio groups, the Hot Fives and Hot Sevens.

The Jazz Tradition

The Twenties and Thirties

By the late 1920s jazz had become a mainstay of American popular dance music and had spread to Europe as well. Black American musicians were touring worldwide, and even in such exotic places as China and India. Wherever they went, their music left a major imprint. Yet there was still quite a gap between jazz at its best and the more commercially acceptable versions of it. Not until the advent of the so-called "Swing Era" did pure jazz reach a level of popular acceptance which, thus far, remains unmatched.

This was due first of all to the big bands, which had reached a new height of artistic maturity. More specifically, it was the result of the efforts of Duke Ellington (1899-1974), rightly called the greatest American composer. Ellington gradually created a perfect balance between written and improvised elements in his unique band, which began an important engagement at Harlem's famous Cotton Club in late 1927. Through appearances there, regular network radio broadcasts, and many recordings, Ellington's music spread rapidly.

Other important work was done by Don Redman and by Benny Carter (1907-), a brilliant multi-instrumentalist and arranger-composer. Fletcher Henderson, who had not previously arranged for his band, began to do so in the early 1930s and soon became one of the best musical arrangers. Such efforts laid the foundation for the success of Benny Goodman (1909-1987), a white clarinetist and band leader, who hired the best black arrangers and was the first white band leader to hire black musicians (including pianist Teddy Wilson in early 1936 and vibraphonist Lionel Hampton later that year).

By 1936 the Swing Era was underway. Black dance styles created at such places as Harlem's Savoy Ballroom swept the nation, and young people jitterbugged to the sounds of an astonishing number of excellent bands, such as those led by Jimmie Lunceford (1902-1947) and Count Basie (1905-1985). The big bands spawned a host of gifted young players and brought into the limelight many giants with established jazz reputations, such as Armstrong, who led his own big bands from 1929 to 1947.

The Postwar Period

Following World War II the singers, whose popularity was first established through their work with the bands, became stars in their own right. The advent of television, which caused more people to find their entertainment at home rather than on the dance floor, also led to a rapid decline of the big bands. Only a handful of these bands survived, among them Ellington's and Basie's.

Meanwhile, the music itself had also undergone fundamental changes. The new generation of players were eager to express themselves at greater length than most big band work permitted. And they were also coming up with new and radical musical ideas.

The most advanced soloists of the Swing Era, such as Roy Eldridge (trumpet), Lester Young (tenor sax), Art Tatum (piano), and

Dizzy Gillespie

Sid Catlett (drums), had been expanding the rhythmic, harmonic, and technical resources of their instruments. Two young geniuses (both doomed to early death by tuberculosis), guitarist Charlie Christian (1916-1942), featured with Benny Goodman, and bassist Jimmy Blanton (1918-1942), featured with Duke Ellington, revolutionized the language of their respective instruments.

Christian was among the many notable players who participated in jam sessions (informal musical get-togethers) at Minton's Playhouse, a nightclub in Harlem, in the early 1940s. The experimentation of musi-cian's at Minton's—where pianist Thelonious Monk and drummer Kenny Clarke were in the regular house band—fed into the new jazz mainstream and led to the advent of modern jazz around 1945.

Bebop

The chief creators of this new jazz language were trumpeter and bandleader-composer Dizzy Gillespie and alto saxophonist composer Charlie "Bird" Parker, both of whom had spent time with leading big bands. While working together in the band of pianist Earl Hines (the father of modern jazz piano style) in 1943, they began to discover their similar musical instincts. When they joined forces in a small group in 1945, bebop (as the new jazz style soon was called) was born.

Though bebop was solidly grounded in earlier jazz styles, it did not seem that way to the public, which often was unable to follow the intricate flourishes of the boppers. Furthermore, the bop musicians, unlike most of the jazz players who preceded them, were not interested in pleasing the public. Instead, they were more concerned with creating music that fulfilled their own ambitions. (Gillespie himself, however, was something of an exception, perhaps because his plentiful sense of humor made him a natural entertainer.)

A New Audience

In any case, the advent of bop went hand in hand with a change in jazz audiences. By the mid-1930s small clubs catering to jazz **connoisseurs** had begun to spring up in most larger urban areas. The biggest and most famous concentration was located in New York, in two blocks on West 52nd Street, which soon became known as "Swing Street." In such clubs, musicians performed for knowledgeable listeners without making musical compromises. By this time, also, many people all over the world had become seriously interested in jazz. Some studied and documented its origins and history, others collected, researched, and classified jazz records. Such publications as *Downbeat* and *Metronome,* in addition, created a strong link between musicians and serious fans.

Bebop was in turn succeeded by more radical forms of jazz, though it has shown

Miles Davis

considerable staying power. In 1959 a young Texas-born alto saxophonist, Ornette Coleman, brought his adventurous quartet to New York and set off a huge controversy with his unusual—and un-jazz-like—music. In fact, Coleman's music was deeply rooted in the blues and in well-established improvisational jazz procedures. In time the Coleman style was accepted as part of the jazz tradition.

The Varied Sounds of Jazz

By then, in the radical 1960s, so-called **avant-garde** jazz was very much in evidence. The trumpeter Miles Davis, who had worked with Charlie Parker and had also led his own influential groups (one of which gave birth to a style known as cool jazz), hired a little-known tenor saxophonist, John Coltrane, in 1956. With Coltrane, who also worked with Thelonious Monk, Davis intro-

John Coltrane

rooted in traditional harmonic ground, expanded solo improvisation dramatically. And by the end of the 1960s, Albert Ayler, a tenor saxophonist with roots in rhythm-and blues music, brought another new and intensely personal voice to jazz.

When Coltrane died suddenly in 1967, jazz was at the height of its experimental, expansionist stage. By then, the term "free jazz" had begun to replace "avant-garde," and many young musicians were following in the footsteps of Coltrane and other innovators. But within a few years of Coltrane's passing, the storm quieted. Despite some later experimentation, jazz by the early 1970s had ended its period of rapid and sometimes almost overpowering development.

In its place came a period of what might be called "peaceful coexistence" of many kinds of jazz. Several young musicians have turned to the rich tradition of jazz for inspiration, among them the gifted trumpeter Wynton Marsalis (also an expert classical player) and several other remarkable musicians from New Orleans, among them Wynton's slightly older brother Branford (a tenor and soprano saxophonist), trumpeter Terence Blanshard, and alto saxophonist Donald Harrison. These young players reject "fusion" with electronics and rock as well as the practices of "free jazz," looking instead to the bebop tradition and even to Armstrong and Ellington for inspiration.

In the late 1980s so-called "repertory jazz" emerged. This refers to the performance of big band compositions and arrangements. The most notable of these ensembles are the Lincoln Center Jazz Orchestra, which specializes in the music of Ellington and features Wynton Marsalis as artistic director; and the

duced an approach based on scales rather than harmonies to jazz improvisation in 1958.

Coltrane soon formed his own group, which took such experiments, both in length and intensity, to a point of near-ecstasy. The pianist Cecil Taylor, a **virtuoso** of the keyboard, further stretched the boundaries of jazz. Davis himself experimented with electronics and rock and soul rhythms. The bassist and composer Charles Mingus, deeply influenced by Ellington and Parker, found new and imaginative ways of combining written and improvised jazz. Tenor saxophonist Sonny Rollins, while remaining

Smithsonian Jazz Masterpiece Ensemble, jointly directed by David Baker and Gunther Schuller, two master musicians with classical as well as jazz training.

The many gifted players who emerged in the 1960s from Chicago's Association for the Advancement of Creative Musicians pursued their various approaches with stirring results in such groups as the Art Ensemble of Chicago, the World Saxophone Quartet, and Lester Bowie's Brass Fantasy.

The Future of Jazz

No one can predict where jazz will go next. After a long and remarkable period of intense innovation, the music seems to have reached a point where it is taking stock of its past while looking ahead. Whatever that future may bring, one thing is certain: the story of jazz is one of the most remarkable chapters in the history of twentieth-century artistic creativity, and the names Armstrong, Ellington, Coltrane, and Parker are bound to loom large when that history is finally written.

Classical

When the first Africans arrived in 1619 on the East Coast of what is now the United States, they brought with them a rich musical heritage. In the culture from which these slaves were torn, music and dance accompanied almost every public activity. Each community had professional musicians and everyone, young and old, played, sang, and danced. Because theirs was an oral tradition, they did not need sheet music to bring their songs and dances with them—they carried it all in their heads. They brought to the new world their songs and dances as well as their love of music as a central part of daily life. From the very beginning, they participated in the music of their new world, enriching it immeasurably over the years.

Slave Music

As slaves, the Africans assumed the lives and culture of their owners, learning Western language, religion, and music. They sang English psalms and hymns in church as they converted to Christianity. They heard folk and popular tunes in the taverns and homes. Some slaves in the South studied with traveling music teachers. The most talented musicians gained professional-level skills that were quickly put to use by the whites.

Both bonded servants and slave musicians, playing instruments such as the violin, flute, and piano, provided much of the recreational music for their masters. They played at dance balls and dancing schools. On the self-sufficient plantation in the South, the most musical of the domestic slaves provided evening "entertainments." Once public concerts became popular in the new world, a few talented slaves were taken on tour. The pianist Thomas "Blind Tom" Green Bethune (1849-1909) began performing for a wide public while still a slave and continued to perform after emancipation.

Art Music in the Nineteenth Century

As a free black middle class arose in the nineteenth century and the popularity of concerts increased, black musicians began to provide "art music" for both black and white audiences. As in white middle- and upper-class communities, polite songs and piano pieces could be heard in the parlors of

Matilda Sissieretta Jones

the comfortable and well-off members of the black communities. Music also accompanied most public celebrations and ceremonies. As these communities grew, they were able to support more professional musicians and music educators. Singing schools and private lessons on instruments were available to anyone interested. During much of the nineteenth century, the best black artists toured throughout the United States and Europe, performing for black and white audiences alike.

In the nineteenth century a typical "art music" concert showcased a variety of musical pieces. Vocalists performed songs, **arias,** and ensemble vocal pieces in the same show as chamber, band, and orchestral numbers. The most popular singers tended to be women such as Elizabeth Taylor Greenfield (c. 1824-1876), called the "Black Swan," and Matilda Sissieretta Jones (1869-1933), also know as the "Black Patti" (a nickname

that referred to the reigning white singer Adelina Patti). African American singers Anna Madah Hyers (1853-1920), Emma Louise Hyers (1855-1890), Sidney Woodward (1860-1924), Nellie Brown Mitchell (1845-1924), Marie Selida (1849-1937), Flora Baston Bergon (1864-1906), Rachel Walker (1873-1940), and Thomas Bowers (1823-1885) all graced the concert stage during the nineteenth century.

Men tended to dominate the realm of instrumental music. Pianists included John William Boone (1864-1927) and Samuel Jamieson (1855-1930). John Thomas Douglas (1847-1886), Walter F. Craig (1854-1920), and Edmond Dede (1877-1903) played the violin. Morris Brown, Jr. (1812-1890), Robert Jones, Jacob Stans, William Appo, James Hermenway (1800-1849), Francis Johnson (1792-1844), and Aaron J. R. Connor conducted all-black orchestras, bands, and choruses. Most composed music as well. The Original Colored American Opera Troupe of Washington, D.C., and the Theodore Drury Colored Opera Company, both established in the second half of the nineteenth century, were the earliest long-lasting black opera companies.

Classical Music in the Twentieth Century

Racism and Sexism in Performance Organizations
During most of the nineteenth century African American musicians performed for both black and white audiences. Towards the end of the century, however, white audiences began to favor European performers over American performers and white musicians over black.

Eleanor Roosevelt resigned from the Daughters of the American Revolution (DAR) and helped arrange for Marian Anderson to sing at the Lincoln Memorial

Despite their obvious success in classical music, African Americans were not considered to be suitable as classical musicians by the beginning of the twentieth century. White audiences accepted blacks only on the vaudeville and minstrel stage, believing them to be unable to contribute to art music as either performer or composer. For example, in response to composer Scott Joplin's attempt to produce his opera *Treemonisha* in New York, the *New York Age* stated on March 5, 1908: "Since ragtime has been in vogue, many Negro writers have gained considerable fame as composers of that style of music. From the white man's stand-point of view ... after writing ragtime, the Negro does not figure." This was the prevailing attitude for some time.

Flutist Dorothy Antoinette Handy (b. 1930) wrote in the preface of her book *Black Women in American Bands and Orchestras* that her book:

> originated in the mind of a fourteen-year-old black American female who decided that she wanted to be a symphonic orchestral flutist.... She went to a New Orleans Philharmonic concert, and shortly before the end proceeded backstage from the reserved for colored section to the orchestra's first flutist. Question: "Are you accepting any pupils?" Answer: "Do you mean that you, a Negro, want to study flute?"

Unfortunately, this attitude has continued to reign in the second half of the century as well. In 1975 San Francisco Symphony Orchestra **timpanist** Elayne Jones, the only black first chair player in a major American orchestra, filed a suit claiming contract violation on grounds of racism and sexism because she was denied **tenure.** She lost her case.

African Americans, despite such opposition, have never been absent from the world of classical music. The merits of their compositions, whether ignored by a broader public or not, are undeniable. For much of this century blacks, though refused entrance to this country's major metropolitan (white) symphonies, have constantly worked towards inclusion.

In 1931 William Grant Still's *Afro-American Symphony* was the first symphon-

Singer Leontyne Price has made numerous appearances at the White House and has performed at two presidential inaugurations

ic work written by a black composer to be performed by a major orchestra, the Rochester Philharmonic Symphony. In 1933 Florence Price duplicated the feat for black women when the Chicago Symphony Orchestra performed her Symphony in E Minor at the Chicago World's Fair. In 1934 Price conducted her Concerto in F Minor in Chicago. And Still became the first African American to conduct a major orchestra in the deep South when, in 1955, he conducted the New Orleans Symphony Orchestra.

The Musical Styles of Black Classical Composers

Black symphonic music falls into two categories: black-stream music, which is serious music influenced by the ethnic background of the composer; and traditional European music created by black composers. At the end of the nineteenth century black composers became the first group of American composers to write nationalistic pieces by including black traditional folk styles in their vocal and instrumental pieces.

Until a few years ago compositions of either style were largely unknown. However, the efforts of researchers and historians have brought to light a great many first-rate symphonic compositions, both old and new. Among the best black-stream pieces are Florence Price's Symphony in E Minor (1933), William Grant Still's *Afro-American Symphony* (1931), Margaret Bond's *Credo,* and Ornette Coleman's *Skies of America.* Examples of black symphonic music in which there is no obvious contribution from the black heritage include Chevalier de Saint Georges's *Symphonic Concertante* (1782), Julia Perry's *Stabat Mater* (1951), and Ulysses Kay's *Markings* (1966).

Research and Recording of Music by Classical Composers

After years of neglect, the role of the African American in the history of music is finally being given serious attention. Rediscoveries of excellent classical pieces by black composers have begun to shatter the stereotype of black music as a limited program of spirituals, jazz, and the blues. Studies of comprehensive musicology (the study of music in relation to the culture and society in which it exists) are beginning to focus on the unique, non-European nature of African American music.

Several new organizations have devoted time, energy, and finances to promoting African American creations and performances in the arts. In 1969 the Afro-American Music Opportunities Association (AAMOA) was formed in order to acknowledge black music and musicians. C. Edward Thomas has developed the organization's concepts into viable and dynamic programs

William Grant Still

that have already changed the study of American music.

The AAMOA issued its own record label for nonsymphonic repertoires with the release of David Baker's *Sonata for Piano and String Quartet* in a performance featuring Brazilian virtuoso Helena Freire. On March 18, 1974, the first four records of the Black Composers Series were formally released by Columbia Records. These discs featured works by Chevalier de Saint-Georges, Samuel Coleridge-Taylor, William Grant Still, George Walker, Ulysses Kay, and Roque Cordero under the artistic direction of Paul Freeman. This Black Composers Series grew out of an agreement between CBS and the AAMOA to create at least 12 recordings of some 20 black composers.

Conductor James DePriest rehearses with the New York Philharmonic Orchestra, 1984

The Center for Black Music Research, established in 1982 at Chicago's Columbia College, has actively contributed to the research and performance of both modern and historic compositions. They have an ever-growing library and computer database of resources used by scholars all over the country. African American classical and popular music has received more attention in the academic world as musicologists, who have been focusing attention in that direction, are beginning to specialize as *ethno*musicologists.

Black and Integrated Performance Organizations

The Symphony of the New World (1965-1976) was established by timpanist Elayne Jones and conductor Benjamin Steinberg as the first racially integrated orchestra in the country. Other founding members included cellist Kermit Moore and bassist Lucille Dixon. This orchestra served as a stepping stone for many of the nation's leading black musicians and composers.

In the 1970s two national black opera companies were formed. Opera/South was founded in 1970 by Sister Elise of the Catholic Order of the Sisters of the Blessed Sacrament and members of the Mississippi Inter-Collegiate Opera Guild (Jackson State University, Utica Junior College, and Tougaloo College). In addition to staging grand opera, the company performed operas by black composers, including *Highway No.*

1 USA and *A Bayou Legend,* both by William Grant Still, and *Jubilee* and *The Juggler of Our Lady,* both by Ulysses Kay. In 1973 Sister Elise, with Margaret Harris, Benjamin Matthews, and Wayne Sanders, organized Opera Ebony. Performers with these two companies have included conductors Leonard de Paur, Margaret Harris, and Everett Lee; pianist Way Sanders; and singers Donnie Ray Albert, William Brown, Alpha Floyed, Ester Hinds, Robert Mosely, Wilma Shakesnider, and Walter Turnbull. These companies, as well as the Houston Opera Company (which in 1975 resurrected Scott Joplin's *Treemonisha*), have served as a showcase for black talent.

Black Representation in Major American Orchestras and Opera Companies

As in other areas of American life, the civil rights struggle continues. Programs that were initiated to support young black artists as a response to the civil rights movements in the 1960s died as a result of the economic recession of the 1970s. A 1981 survey by the National Urban League disclosed that of the nearly 5,000 musicians playing regularly in 56 leading orchestras, only 70 were black. Only 6 of the 538 members of the "Big Five"

orchestras (New York, Boston, Chicago, Cleveland, and Philadelphia) were black. Few employ black conductors. The American Symphony Orchestra League published a report in 1992 with similar findings. The 146 orchestras that participated in the survey reported that of a total 8,326 positions, only 133 were filled by black musicians.

In the early 1980s the Metropolitan Opera had 15 black artists on its roster, and the New York City Opera had 11 singers in principal roles with 2 conductors and 1 stage director. Prior to World War II, there were no black singers in any opera house in the United States, but now they are accepted almost everywhere.

The Future for the Black Classical Musicians

It is impossible to know what lies in the future for African American classical composers, conductors, and other performing artists. Certainly the music of African Americans has been increasingly accepted and celebrated by both the musical and academic worlds, and the formation of the companies mentioned above has provided an avenue for blacks to embrace classical music and to continue to shape its development.

23

Fine and Applied Arts

The African American Artist

FACT FOCUS

- Joshua Johnston was the first black portrait painter to win recognition in America.
- Edmonia Lewis was the first nationally recognized African American woman artist.
- In 1927 Henry Ossawa Tanner became the first black artist to gain full membership in the National Academy.
- Howard University established its first art gallery, under the directorship of James V. Herrings, in 1930.
- Selma Burke was the first black sculptor to design a United States coin. She won a competition to design the portrait of Franklin D. Roosevelt that appeared on the dime.

"Can't nothin' make your life work if you ain't the architect."—Terry McMillan

"The life of the Negro community is bound to enter a new dynamic phase, the buoyancy from within compensating for whatever pressure there may be of conditions from without."—Alain Locke, The New Negro *(1925)*

Blacks in the United States and in Europe were long cut off from the artistic heritage of Africa, a heritage now known for its tremendous achievements. As black scholar Alain Locke pointed out in 1931, "the liberating example" of African art was used by white Europeans long before it reached African Americans.

From colonial times to the present, black artistic talent has been encouraged and recognized on a very limited basis in the United States. However, some white institutions, such as the Rosenwald Fund in the early twentieth century, did help finance promising blacks. More support came later from the Harmon, Rockefeller, Guggenheim, and Whitney foundations and from government programs, such as the Works Project Administration (WPA) and the National Endowment for the Arts. State Arts Councils, formed in the 1960s and 1970s, have also provided grants for artists. The need for support, however, has always been greater than the amount of sponsorships available.

Early African American themes and expressions—whether related to slave, sharecropper, or ghetto life—have rarely been regarded as prime attractions by leading **curators** of the art world. Until very recently, few blacks had attained the economic security and leisure essential to creativity and **patronage** of artists. Art history books include the contributions of one or two African American artists and very little about African art, although images of blacks abound in ancient paintings, **mosaics,** and sculpture. If Africans were subjects, is it not reasonable to assume that they were also artists?

Black Artists in Early America

In the eighteenth century the first known African American artists worked in a variety of **fine** and **applied arts,** from clay sculpting to metal casting. Unfortunately, the only eighteenth-century African American artist who left a historical record was Scipio Morehead. Morehead's artwork appears to have been aided by two women who lived in Boston where he was a slave. One was his master's wife and the other was poet Phillis Wheatley, who was herself a slave. Morehead's style was likely **neoclassical,** in keeping with the period, and resembled the work of British masters George Romney and Sir Joshua Reynolds. Although no major work of Morehead is known to have survived, a small portrait of Phillis Wheatley is believed to be his.

Certainly there were other black artists and craftsmen in the eighteenth century who have left little trace in history. Records indicate that skilled blacks interested in buying their freedom worked as painters, silversmiths, cabinet and coach makers, ornamen-

---

WORDS TO KNOW

aesthetics: the study or theory of beauty as it relates to art

applied arts: fields in which art serves a dual function, such as graphic or fashion design

curators: heads of museums or special collections

fine arts: fields in which art stands alone, such as painting or sculpture

mosaics: pictures composed of small bits of stone, glass, tile, etc.

negritude: the awareness among blacks of their cultural heritage

neoclassical: art or literature dating from the mid-seventeenth to mid-eighteenth century that revived the classic forms and styles of ancient Greece and Rome

patronage: support, usually monetary

philanthropist: one who offers **patronage,** a humanitarian

retrospectives: exhibits that look back at an artist's development

---

talists, and shipwrights. For example, Eugene Warbourg, a black sculptor from New Orleans, became well known for his ornamental gravestones and eventually went to study in Europe. And Bill Day, a celebrated carpenter, gained recognition for his interior design as well as his furniture. Finally, much colonial iron work and metal work on eighteenth-century mansions, churches, and public buildings was created by blacks. Some of it has since been classified as fine art.

Newspaper Boy, by Edward Mitchell Bannister, 1869

Emerging African American artists in the eighteenth and nineteenth centuries found that their cultural roots were ignored; to become professionals they had to copy European artistic styles. Many were trained by white artists and traveled to Europe to study. Although their works received some degree of popular acceptance, these artists were kept out of the mainstream by racism. Even so, most continued to work in the United States in spite of their status, and some were able to overcome tremendous obstacles to win recognition for their art. Among these were Edward Mitchell Bannister, Robert Duncanson, Meta Warrick Fuller, Joshua Johnston, Edmonia Lewis, and Henry Ossawa Tanner.

Some African American artists escaped the classical tradition and painted themes closer to their heritage and existence. For example, Henry Ossawa Tanner's paintings in the 1880s of poor blacks stem from this unheralded school of African American art.

By the turn of the century, most African American artists continued to look toward western Europe for their themes and development of expression; few demonstrated an ethnic awareness.

Hagar in the Wilderness, by Edmonia Lewis

Meta Warrick Fuller's bronze *Water Boy,* in the National Archives, Washington, D.C.

Two important developments in art helped to change this. The first was the 1913 Armory Show of works by European Cubist and Modernist painters. These artists revealed an interest in, and influence from, African abstraction of form. The second was the growing interest among American art circles in subjects tied to social issues. Both developments opened the doors to new interpretations and values in artistic expression.

During this transition period many blacks traveled to Europe to study, believing that the artistic climate there was most open to free experimentation and expression. Their art began to display personal dignity and ethnic awareness. The artists of this period —Palmer Hayden, Archibald Motley, Malvin Gray Johnson, William Edouard Scott, Meta Warrick Fuller, and Laura Wheeler Waring—were among the major contributors to this new trend.

African American Artists in the Harlem Renaissance

The respect for **negritude** and African styles that began to appear after World War I can be traced directly to cultural activities that developed in several important cities during the 1920s, notably Cleveland, Chicago, and New York.

Especially important was the founding of Karamu House in Cleveland in 1915. A center for cultural activities, Karamu fostered such artists as Hughie Lee-Smith, Zell Ingrams, Charles Sallee, Elmer Brown, William E. Smith, and George Hulsinger. In 1927 **philanthropist** William E. Harmon established the Harmon Foundation to aid African American artists. The foundation offered financial awards, sponsored shows, and encouraged the growth of art education programs in many black institutions throughout the country. The Harmon Foundation became one of the major organizations involved in the protection and presentation of African American art in the United States and continued to exist until the mid-1960s.

The 1930s brought the Great Depression and the Works Project Administration (WPA.) Black artists abandoned by the white philanthropists of the 1920s were rescued by the WPA. Under this program, Aaron Douglas, Augusta Savage, Charles Alston, Hale Woodruff, and Charles White created murals and other works for public buildings. In 1939 the Baltimore Museum

A mural by Hale Woodruff depicting the contribution of African Americans in the history of California

Show, the first show of African American artists to be held in a Southern region, presented the works of Richmond Barthe, Malvin Gray Johnson, Henry Bannarn, Florence Purviance, Hale Woodruff, Dox Thrash, Robert Blackburn, and Archibald Motley. The Harlem Art Center and the Chicago South Side Community Art Center also began with the WPA.

Artistic portrayals of the African American became very important in the first three decades of this century. At the urging of Alain Locke, W. E. B. Du Bois, and others, creative artists began working together in literature, music, theater, and art to promote an important cultural heritage. Aaron Douglas was considered the leading painter of "The Negro Renaissance." Active in New York from 1923 to 1925, Douglas was the first to portray visual symbols—African fig-

ures with overlays of geometric forms that created movement and rhythm. The idea spread beyond Harlem, where many artists had settled from the Caribbean and other parts of the United States. Promoting ethnic awareness and pride, this movement shattered the stereotypes and shallow interpretations common in the popular culture.

African American Artists since the Depression

During this period artists continued to depict the American social and political climate from an African American point of view. World War II seemed to bring a sense of urgency to the search for equality. When the armed services were integrated, black Americans hoped for equality in other areas of life. There was a great migration from the

Romare Bearden's *Pepper Jelly Lady*

South to Northern cities, documented by artists such as Romare Bearden, Benford Delaney, Jacob Lawrence, and Hughie Lee-Smith. African Americans in search of self and a better life characterized much of the art of the 1940s and 1950s.

The influence of previous decades was evident in the continuation of muralist art. In her book *Art: African American* (Handcraft Studios, Los Angeles, California), Samella Lewis notes that exterior murals are an important element in many African architectural traditions. Charles Alston, John Biggers, Jacob Lawrence, and Charles White became important muralists during this period. Inspired by Mexican mural artists (who championed social change through their art), African American artists were especially drawn to the themes, bold forms, and bright colors of such artists as Diego Rivera, David Alfero Siqueiros, and Jose Clemente Orozco.

Conscious of the need to study the history, **aesthetics,** and formal qualities of art, African American artists continued to venture abroad to Paris, Rome, and, before the war, Germany. However, most stayed at home and attended classes at such universities as Columbia (in New York City), Ohio State, and Pennsylvania State or such professional art schools as the Art Institute of Chicago, the New York Art Students' League, and the Philadelphia Academy of Art. Black institutions such as Fisk, Hampton Institute, Howard, Morehouse, and Tuskegee emphasized art education as a means of survival and encouraged defining future black culture and values through the visual arts.

In the 1940s more African Americans were being awarded art degrees than ever before. Some turned to abstraction and to non-objective art (as did, for example, Delilah Pierce); others sought expressive forms such as those in many works by Norman Lewis who, for a time, was a part of the group known as the Action Painters. (Jackson Pollock, a white artist, was a member of the Action Painters and listened to jazz as he worked.) Romare Bearden studied Cubism, as did Aaron Douglas. Early on, long before American critics would write about it, they knew the African roots of this art form.

As Jim Crow laws began to crumble in the South, black artists were there to document, to inspire, and to champion the "cause." As barriers to racial equality slowly broke down, the period was marked by social unrest. Social and political expressions dominated the African American artistic world. However, those artists who thought that art should be separate from race and politics also continued to create. Horace Pippin, William Edmonson, and Clementine Hunter, who were self-taught individuals, and E. Simms Campbell, cartoonist and successful pictorial journalist for *Esquire* and the *New Yorker,* were among them.

The Search for an African American Identity

The search for a black identity and the expression of black militancy were the most widespread themes of black art in the 1960s. Sometimes emotions could not be contained on canvas or channeled into familiar forms. Because of this, art literally took to the streets of the ghetto to meet with, appeal to, and celebrate the people; this was richly illustrated in the murals of Chicago and Detroit.

In New York City in 1972, armed with spray paint and street pride, African American and Hispanic teenagers created a colorful art form called "wall graffiti." Often wall graffiti consists of no more than the name of a street gang or the nickname of the individual painter; it may also include the name or number of the street on which the artist lives, or to which he or she is loyal. On the other hand, the paintings may be highly detailed, with cartoon characters and lavish lettering. Toward the end of the 1970s and well into the 1980s, this graffiti style became more and more popular and valuable, and several of the young street artists were welcomed into the mainstream art world. One young artist who became a superstar was Jean-Michel Basquiat.

A number of mainstream artists, including Keith Haring, made the graffiti style their own, and galleries such as the Paula Cooper Gallery opened their doors to this new and defiant art. Choreographer Twyla Tharp created a ballet for the Joffrey Company titled *Deuce Coupe* in which dancers moved against a background provided by spray-can-armed boys painting on sheets of paper hung from the ceiling.

In the 1990s multimedia art forms employing videos and computers came to the forefront. Artists also began experimenting with various artform combinations as well as new artistic arenas, including the environment, factories, and school buildings. Stones, hair, elephant dung, twigs, bricks, discards, and other odd objects often replaced traditional materials. Words, symbols, and numbers as images took on a new emphasis, as did the actual gestures of performance artists.

Art in the 1990s is interested in how groups of people see themselves and others. An African American identity continues to evolve, nurtured by a climate of sharing among Native, African, Asian, European, and Hispanic American cultures.

Architecture and the Applied Arts

Architecture

Africans brought to America many building skills, including metalworking, woodcarving, masonry, and toolmaking. They built dwellings in Virginia and other parts of the Americas like rondavels found in Mali, Africa. These round brick slave quarters were topped with conical roofs and date from the eighteenth century. In the nineteenth century they built homes now called "shotgun houses," a part of the legacy from the Yoruba people of Western Africa. These mostly urban houses were narrow dwellings 10 to 14 feet wide, with two or more rooms, varying in length from 22 to 65 feet, and with ceilings from 6 to 12 feet in height. Slaves also built many mansions and public buildings. One built entirely by slaves was a courthouse in Vicksburg, Mississippi, which later became a museum.

Like other Africans before and after emancipation, black tradespeople interested in technology and art sought to copy their European counterparts and were trained as slave laborers or apprentices. In time, they too began to craft original works in wood, wrought and cast iron, and other materials.

The first black to receive a degree from the Massachusetts Institute of Technology was architect Robert Taylor in 1892. Later, at Tuskegee Institute, Taylor opened the first school of architecture in a black university. In 1901 John A. Lankford designed and oversaw the construction of the Pythian Building, an office and social building completed entirely by African Americans.

The first African American to be accepted into the American Institute of Architects was Paul R. Williams (1926); the first African American woman to be elected was Norma Merrick Sklarek (1966). Today there are over 800 registered architects in the United States who are African American.

In 1991 New York architect Jack Travis edited *African-American Architects in Current Practice* a book on 33 outstanding African American architects that also includes a chronology of African Americans in architecture since 1868 compiled by Vinson McKenzie of Auburn University in Auburn, Alabama. (The book is published by Princeton Architectural Press.)

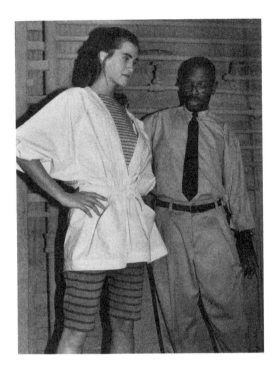

Willi Smith

The Applied Arts: Crafts, Illustration, Fashion Design, and Automobile Design

The artistic heritage of African Americans includes dressmaking and tailoring, quilting, weaving, silversmithing, engraving, and ceramic production, as well as jewelrymaking, stitchery, stained-glass production, glassblowing, mosaic construction, and enameling. Many slaves learned their crafts in Africa. As these skills were discovered, the slave masters put these workers to specialized use and trained their slaves in new skills as needed.

The twentieth century saw a revival of functional art. There was a great crafts revival, and many artists began to employ traditional crafts methods and materials in

1993 Oldsmobile Achieva SC, designed by Edward T. Welburn

their art. Because of this, the line between art and craft has practically disappeared.

In illustration, graphic artists Jerry Pinkney and Larry Johnson are examples of successful African Americans who have used their skills to design postage stamps, children's books, editorial cartoons, and illustrations for other publications. African American artists in fashion design include Stephen Burrows, Gordon Henderson, and Willi Smith. In automobile design, Emeline King and Edward T. Welburn are successful artists. Careers in industrial design, unlike in the previous century, are filled by trained artists who combine engineering studies with art.

Museums and Galleries since the 1960s

In the 1960s the United States underwent radical social and cultural upheaval. African Americans throughout the country were demanding political, social, and cultural recognition. No longer satisfied with the limited support of such organizations as the Harmon Foundation, these artists looked for different forms of exposure; as a result, galleries, community art centers, and community art galleries flourished.

New York City

In New York City the Acts of Art Gallery was established in 1969—by Nigel Jackson, a former artist turned administrator—providing exhibition space for contemporary artists. A nonprofit organization, the gallery was dedicated to promoting these artists and providing them with the opportunity to attract collectors interested in their work. The gallery shows included the works of

James Van Der Zee recorded the visual history of Harlem over the course of a half-century

such artists as James Denmark, Dinga Mc-Cannon, Frank Wimberly, Ann Tanksley, Don Robertson, Lloyd Toomes, Lois Mailou Jones, Jo Butler, Robert Threadgill, and Faith Ringgold.

The Studio Museum in Harlem began in 1969 under the direction of Edward Spriggs. Set up as a place for artists who needed working space, it eventually branched out into a cultural center where the artists could display their work, meet other artists and art supporters, and hold concerts, panel discussions, and other art-related activities. By 1972 the Studio Museum in Harlem had become the New York African American community's cultural center. Important **retrospectives** included the works of Palmer Hayden, Hale Woodruff, Beauford Delaney, Bob Thompson, and James Van Der Zee. In January 1988 the Museum's deputy director, Kinshasha Holman Conwill, wife of artist Houston Conwill, was named director. The Studio Museum has continued to expand its audience, exhibitions, and programs.

Just Above Midtown Gallery was the first organization to move into the gallery district in New York City. Established in 1976, it set up its operation base in a modest space on 57th Street in midtown Manhattan. Under the directorship of Linda Bryant, the organization presented many of the leading contemporary artists of the 1970s, including David Hammons, Senga Nengudi, Randy Williams, and Howardena Pindell. Bryant aimed to place African American artists in direct competition with mainstream American artists. No longer could art critics refuse to review these works because they could not get to Harlem, Queens, or Brooklyn. But the cost of running a gallery took its toll and in order to continue operations Bryant was forced to turn the gallery into a nonprofit organization, adding educational programs for young artists, music concerts, performance programs, slide reviews, and lectures.

By the end of 1979 Just Above Midtown moved from 57th Street to a larger space on Franklin Street in the Tribeca section of New York, changed its name to the Just Above Midtown/Downtown Alternative Art Center, and opened its doors to new-wave artists.

The Schomburg Center for Research in Black Culture of the New York Public Library is one of the most widely used research facilities on black life in the world.

The Center first won international acclaim in 1926 when the personal collection of black scholar Arthur A. Schomburg was added to the Division of Negro Literature, History and Prints of the 135th Street Branch of the New York Public Library. Schomburg's collection included over 5,000 volumes, 3,000 manuscripts, 2,000 etchings and paintings, and several thousand pamphlets. Today, the Schomburg Center is the guardian of over 5,000,000 items and provides a wide variety of services and programs.

The Cinqué Gallery was the concept of three distinguished artists—Romare Bearden, Norman Lewis, and Ernest Crichlow. Opened in 1969, the gallery was named after the famous African slave Joseph Cinqué, who in 1839 led a successful revolt aboard the slave ship *Amistad,* won his freedom, and returned to Africa. Bearden, Crichlow, and Lewis sought to establish an exhibition space specifically for young African American artists who needed to learn how to become professional artists. By the end of the 1970s the gallery doors opened to all new and emerging artists regardless of age.

The Hatch-Billops Studio, named after the husband-wife team of Camille Billops and Jim Hatch, began in New York in 1968 as an organization designed to present multiethnic plays, performances, and exhibitions. By 1973 the studio began collecting third world memorabilia. Around the same time, Billops and Hatch began taping the personal histories of some black theater artists. Today the collection houses more than 600 taped interviews and panel and media events about or by artists. There are well over 10,000 slides and 3,000 books, clippings, files, letters, memorabilia, programs, photographs, drawings, scrapbooks, and videotapes. This collection—available to artists, scholars, and students—is one of the most complete reference centers focusing on African American visual, literary, and theatrical art.

Other Locales

Galleries and museums for African American artists were developing throughout the country. In Los Angeles, Samella Lewis, a painter, art historian, and professor at Claremont College, founded the Contemporary Craft Center. Alonzo and Dale Davis established and directed the Brockman Galleries Productions, a nonprofit gallery showing contemporary African American art and the work of other minority artists.

In Chicago, the Du Sable Museum was established in 1961 under the directorship of Margaret Burroughs to provide the South Side community with an art center. The museum grew out of an art center that was established under the Works Project Administration during the Depression. Some of the artists presented there include Charles White, Elizabeth Catlett, Gordon Parks, Rex Gorleigh, William McBride, Jr., and Eldzier Cortor.

In Boston, the museum of the National Center of Afro-American Artists, begun in 1969 under the curatorship of Edmond Barry Gaither, is a multimedia art center featuring dance, theater, visual arts, film, and educational programs.

In Washington, D.C., the Museum of African Art, formerly known as the Frederick Douglass Institute, was established in 1964 and until 1984 existed in a Victorian row house on Capitol Hill, nestled in the

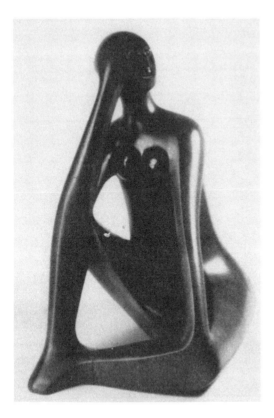

Elizabeth Catlett's *Woman Resting*

shadow of the United States Supreme Court. The house once belonged to Frederick Douglass, a former slave who became an advisor to President Lincoln. In 1984 the museum was moved to the Smithsonian Institute; the house, dedicated to early African American art and memorabilia, continues to be known as the Frederick Douglass Institute.

The museum was established to familiarize Americans with the artistic heritage of Africa. Today it includes one of the largest and most diverse collections of its kind in the country, consisting of some 65,000 works, including traditional carvings, musical instruments, and textiles with a special focus on works from Nigeria, Ghana, Liberia, the Ivory Coast, and Zaire.

Black Milestones and Major Black Exhibits

During the late 1960s and early 1970s leading mainstream museums began to respond to demands that they hire African American scholars as curators and administrators. At the time of the demonstrations, Kynastan McShine, a young West Indian who had already established his reputation as a strong curator at the Jewish Museum, moved on to become the assistant curator of painting and sculpture at the Museum of Modern Art. Howardena Pindell had just begun her career at the Museum of Modern Art as the assistant curator of drawings and prints. She would later move on to become the associate curator before pursuing her own career as an artist. However, such examples of progress were not satisfactory to the artists who demonstrated and wrote letters demanding that jobs be made available to black art historians.

In 1968 Gylbert Coker became the first African American to be hired at the Guggenheim Museum in an administrative trainee position. She later went on to work at the Museum of Modern Art as cataloguer in the museum's registration department. In 1976 she received the Rockefeller Fellowship in Museum Education and spent one year at the Metropolitan Museum of Art. The following year she became the curator of the Studio Museum in Harlem where she set up their registration department and organized such important shows as the Bob Thompson Exhibition and the Hale Woodruff Retrospective before leaving to pursue a career as a free-lance critic and curator.

In 1980 and again in 1982 Coker codirected *Art Across the Park,* an outdoor exhibition created by the artist David Hammons. The project was so popular that several groups in New York tried to copy the concept. It was the first large-scale exhibit that openly encouraged all artists to take part, and it was during this show that the term *multi-ethnic* was coined.

Cheryl McClenny was the second African American to work at the Guggenheim in an administrative position. She went on to direct the Museum Collaborative Programs for the City of New York and, in 1978, became an administrator with the National Endowment for the Arts in Washington, D.C. In 1980 she was appointed director of the Philadelphia Museum of Art.

From the Whitney Museum's Museum Studies Program came Faith Weaver and Horace Brockington. Faith Weaver went on to teach American Art History at the School of Visual Arts. Brockington gained renown for his show *Another Generation* for the Studio Museum in Harlem in 1978, which set the stage for *African-American Abstraction,* presented two years later at P.S. 1, an alternative art center. The Brooklyn Museum opened its Community Gallery and hired Henri Ghent, who began to produce some very important exhibitions, including several African American shows that were sent to Europe.

The Metropolitan Museum of Art in New York City sponsored the largest such community program. There, Randy Williams, Florence Hardney, Dolores Wright, Cathy Chance, Lowery Sims, and others actively

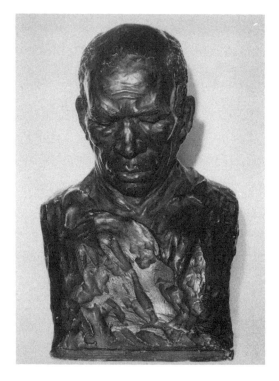

A bust by Richmond Barthe

presented the art works of African American and other minority artists to the Metropolitan Museum's audience. By 1977 Lowery Sims was made the museum's first black assistant curator within the museum's Twentieth-Century Department, under the guidance of Henry Geldzahler. She later became the associate curator under William Leiberman.

Regina Perry was invited by the Metropolitan Museum of Art in 1976 to produce a show called *Selections of Nineteenth-Century Afro-American Art.* It was an exhibition that for the first time highlighted many early African American portrait painters and landscape artists; it also attempted to document slave artifacts as important early artwork.

Abraham's Oak, by Henry Ossawa Tanner, 1905

Also in 1976 Lowery Sims put together a show of selected works by twentieth-century black artists from the museum's collection for the Bedford-Stuyvesant Restoration Corporation. Three years later Sims mounted another exhibition of African American paintings from the twentieth-century collection. This time the show was held within the Metropolitan Museum.

The Newark Museum of Art in New Jersey held its first black exhibition in 1944. The show included the works of Richmond Barthe, Romare Bearden, and William Edmonson. Thirty years later, in 1974, the museum presented its second African American art exhibit, *Black Artists: Two Generations.* The curator was Paul Waters.

By the 1990s mainstream museums across the country (including those in Brooklyn, Hartford, Detroit, Atlanta, Dallas, San Francisco, and Seattle) were sponsoring major exhibits of the works of African American artists and were also displaying collections and artifacts designed to appeal to black audiences.

Facing History: The Black Image in American Art, 1710-1940 was a major exhibit curated by Guy C. McElroy, who also wrote a catalogue with an essay by Henry Louis Gates, Jr. It was shown in Washington, D.C., at the Corcoran Gallery of Art and in Brooklyn, New York, at the Brooklyn Museum in 1990. The Wadsworth Atheneum in Hartford, Connecticut, opened its African American Gallery with an exhibit from the National Museum of American Art, *Free Within Ourselves: African-American Art in the Collection of the National Museum of American Art*. The catalogue was written by Regina Perry of the National Museum of American Art and the show was curated by Linda Roscoe Hartigan.

In 1989 the Dallas Museum organized *Black Art: Ancestral Legacy* with an impressive staff that included Alia J. Wardlaw, chief curator; Regina Perry and Barry Gaither, curators; and David Boxer, David C. Driskell, William Ferris, and Robert Ferris Thompson, advisors. The catalogue was edited by Robert V. Rozelle, Alia Wardlaw,

and Maureen A. Mckenna, project director (Dallas Museum of Art/Abrams, 1989).

The Seattle Museum launched a major retrospective in 1986 of the work of Jacob Lawrence, often referred to as the "Dean of Black Painters"; the retrospective was still being shown in major museums in 1993. In 1991 the Philadelphia Museum of Art organized a retrospective of the works of its native son, Henry Ossawa Tanner. One hundred years earlier, Tanner left the United States to live and paint in Paris.

Major funders of these exhibits included the National Endowment of the Arts, private charities and foundations, state and local arts commissions, universities, and such corporations as IBM, Ford Motor Co., and Philip Morris Corp. If museums can continue to attract money while serving the public at large, there is no doubt that African American art will continue to enter the mainstream.

24

Science, Medicine, and Invention

African American Contributions to Science

FACT FOCUS

- Lucas Santomee was the first trained African American doctor.
- Augustus Jackson of Philadelphia invented ice cream in 1832.
- Susan McKinney Steward was the first black woman to be formally certified as a doctor.
- Elijah McCoy was known for his inventions related to the lubrication of engines. Some 57 *patents* were granted to him during his career.
- In 1883 Jan Matzeliger revolutionized the shoe industry with his patented lasting machine, which speeded the production of shoes as much as 14 times over hand-sewn methods.
- The first known black woman inventor is Sarah E. Goode, who patented a folding cabinet bed in 1885.
- In 1891 Daniel Hale Williams founded Provident Hospital in Chicago as a facility to serve people of all races.
- Eva B. Dykes, Sadie T. Mosell, and Georgiana Rose Simpson were the first black women to receive doctor's degrees.
- The gas mask and the traffic light were invented by Garrett Morgan.
- David H. Blackwell became the first African American member of the National Academy of Sciences in 1965.

"The color of the skin is in no ways connected with strength of the mind or intellectual power."—Benjamin Banneker, Banneker's Almanac *(1796)*

Most of America's earliest African American scientists and inventors are largely unknown, though their contributions live on, contributing to the fabric of American culture. Maryland-born Benjamin Banneker is one of the few black names that has survived in histories of American science and invention. His eighteenth-century successes in timepieces and urban planning are generally known and applauded. Nevertheless, we

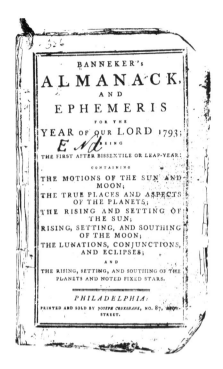

Benjamin Banneker, America's first black scientist and probably the inventor of the first clock made in America, was also known for his almanacs and for his help in planning the layout of Washington, D.C.

WORDS TO KNOW

glaucoma: an eye-related disorder that can, if untreated, cause a total loss of vision

inoculation: an injection, aimed at disease prevention, that causes a mild form of the disease; the injection forces the body to build up an immunity to a later attack of the actual disease

patents: legal and exclusive rights to produce, use, and sell what one has invented

plasma: the fluid part of blood

predecessors: those who have gone before, usually said of influential persons

syphilis: a venereal, or sexually transmitted, disease that can lead to a weakening of the bones, nerve tissue, and heart

cannot identify many achievements of seventeenth- and eighteenth-century blacks in architecture, agriculture, and masonry.

While historians increasingly recognize that blacks had a significant impact on the design and construction of plantations and public buildings in the South and that rice farming in the Carolinas might not have been possible without blacks, the identities of individuals who spearheaded these accomplishments remain a mystery.

Early Scientists and Inventors

Before the Civil War slaves could not obtain patents, either for themselves or their owners. Slaves were not recognized as citizens and therefore could not enter into contracts with their owners or the government. As a result, the efforts of slaves were either dismissed or, if accepted, they were credited entirely to their masters.

Although we know that African Americans worked on significant inventions, we can only guess at what role they actually played. Take, for example, the grain harvester of Cyrus McCormick. Jo Anderson, one of McCormick's slaves, is believed to have played a major role in the creation of the McCormick harvester, but records of the period give few answers.

The inventions of free blacks were, how-

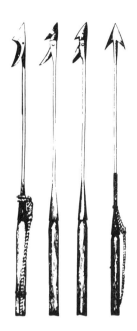

The toggle harpoon, invented by Lewis Temple

(Granville Woods, 1888); and an automatic railroad car coupler (Andrew Beard, 1897).

Scientists and Inventors in the Twentieth Century

The contributions of African American scientists are better known than those of black inventors, partly because of the recognition awarded George Washington Carver, an agricultural scientist who, strangely enough, refused to patent most of his inventions. Moreover, black scientists contributed significantly to the development of blood **plasma,** open heart surgery, the treatment of **glaucoma,** and the development of cortisone, all vital ingredients of modern health care.

George Washington Carver

ever, recorded. Henry Blair—who was awarded a patent for a corn planter in 1934 —was probably the first black granted a patent. But again, records fail the historian, for the race of inventors was rarely noted. Blair may well have had numerous **predecessors.** Other black inventions were not patented for various reasons, as was the case with ice cream, invented by Augustus Jackson of Philadelphia in 1832.

The Reconstruction era unleashed the creativity that had been suppressed in blacks. Between 1870 and 1900 blacks were awarded several hundred patents. Notable among these were the shoe last (Jan Matzeliger, 1883); a machine for making paper bags (William Purvis, 1884); assorted machinery-lubricating equipment (Elijah McCoy, from 1872 on); a railroad telegraph

INVENTIONS

Following are a number of devices invented by African Americans:

Inventor	Invention	Date
Betsy Ancker Johnson	Signal generator	November 22, 1966
A. P. Ashborne	Biscuit cutter	November 30, 1875
William Bailes	Ladder scaffold-support	August 5, 1879
L. C. Bailey	Folding bed	July 18, 1899
R. G. Bayliss & D. D. Emrick	Encapsulation process	February 2, 1971
A. J. Beard	Rotary engine	July 5, 1892
L. Bell	Locomotive smokestack	May 23, 1871
A. B. Blackburn	Railway signal	January 10, 1888
Henry Blair	Corn planter	October 14, 1834
G. S. Bluford, Sr.	Artillery ammunition training round	February 13, 1951
Sarah Boone	Ironing board	April 26, 1892
C. B. Brooks	Street-sweeper	March 17, 1896
O. E. Brown	Horseshoe	August 23, 1892
J. A. Burr	Lawnmower	May 9, 1899
W. F. Burr	Switching device for railways	October 31, 1899
T. A. Carrington	Range	July 25, 1876
W. C. Carter	Umbrella stand	August 4, 1885
J. L. Carter, M. Weiner & R. J. Youmans	Distributed pulse forming network for magnetic modulator	September 16, 1986
M. A. Cherry	Street car fender	January 1, 1895
O. B. Clare	Trestle	October 9, 1888
J. Cooper	Elevator device	April 2, 1895
W. D. Davis	Riding saddle	October 6, 1896
W. A. Deitz	Shoe	April 30, 1867
C. J. Dorticus	Photographic print wash	April 23, 1875
P. B. Downing	Electric switch for railroads	June 17, 1890
T. Elkins	Refrigerating apparatus	November 4, 1879
F. Flemming, Jr.	Guitar (variation)	March 3, 1886
J. Forten	Sail control	c. 1850
G. F. Grant	Golf tee	December 12, 1899
R. H. Gray	Bailing press	August 28, 1894
Lloyd A. Hall	Apparatus for sterilizing foodstuff	February 8, 1938
Solomon Harper	Electric hair treatment	August 5, 1930
J. H. Hunter	Portable weighing scales	November 3, 1896
B. F. Jackson	Gas burner	April 4, 1899
W. H. Jackson	Railway switch	March 9, 1897
I. R. Johnson	Bicycle frame	October 10, 1899

INVENTIONS

Following are a number of devices invented by African Americans:

Inventor	Invention	Date
W. Johnson	Egg beater	February 5, 1884
F. M. Jones	Air conditioning unit	July 12, 1949
Hubert Julian	Airplane safety device	May 24, 1921
L. H. Latimer	Lamp fixture	August 10, 1910
W. Lavalette	Printing press (variation)	September 17, 1878
E. Little	Bridle-bit	March 7, 1882
J. L. Love	Pencil sharpener	November 23, 1897
W. A. Martin	Lock	July 23, 1889
E. McCoy	Lubricator for steam engines	July 2, 1872
A. Miles	Elevator	October 11, 1887
W. U. Moody	Game board design	May 11, 1897
G. W. Murray	Planter	June 5, 1894
S. Newson	Oil heater or cooker	May 22, 1894
John Perry, Jr. & H. F. Hunger	Biochemical fuel cell	November 8, 1966
J. F. Pickering	Air ship	February 20, 1900
Al. G. B. Prather	Man-powered glider aircraft	February 6, 1973
W. B. Purvis	Fountain pen	January 7, 1890
R. R. Reynolds	Nonrefillable bottle	May 2, 1899
A. C. Richardson	Churn	February 17, 1891
C. V. Richey	Fire escape bracket	December 28, 1897
G. T. Sampson	Clothes drier	June 7, 1892
S. R. Scottron	Curtain rod	August 30, 1892
R. B. Spikes	Automatic gear shift	December 6, 1932
R. B. Spikes	Multiple barrel machine gun	c. 1940
J. Standard	Refrigerator	July 14, 1891
E. H. Sutton	Cotton cultivator	April 7, 1878
B. H. Taylor	Rotary engine	April 23, 1878
L. Temple	Toggle harpoon	c. 1848
S. E. Thomas	Casting	July 31, 1888
S. E. Thomas	Pipe connection	October 9, 1888
George Toliver	Propeller for vessels	April 28, 1891
Wade Washington	Corn husking machine	August 14, 1883
F. H. West	Weather shield	September 5, 1899
G. T. Woods	Telephone transmitter (variation)	December 2, 1884
G. T. Woods	Railway telegraphy	November 15, 1887
James Wormley	Lifesaving apparatus	May 24, 1881

The achievements of black inventors and scientists of the mid-twentieth century have been overlooked for reasons beyond racial prejudice, among them the replacement of the individual inventor by government and corporate research and development teams. Individuals, whatever their race, receive less recognition. The creators of such mid-twentieth-century inventions as the computer, television, heart pacers, and lasers are relatively obscure, while every school child learns such names as Alexander Graham Bell and Thomas Edison.

In recent years an increasing number of black students have demonstrated an interest in science, especially so since the death of Major Robert H. Lawrence, America's first black astronaut. Already, African American scientists and engineers are a crucial part of the National Aeronautic and Space Administration (NASA). In the corporate and university worlds, African American scientists and engineers play a substantial role in the development of solid state devices, high-powered and ultra fast lasers, hypersonic flight, and elementary particle science.

African American engineers employed at NASA in managerial and research positions have made and continue to make considerable contributions. However, government research work often limits individual recognition since such projects are frequently done in groups or in teams.

Yet, there are increasing opportunities for black achievement in the sciences. African American manufacturing and servicing firms in various computer and engineering areas are springing up and expanding. And today there are more African American science and technology faculty members, college presidents, and school of engineering deans than ever before. Many of these academics are serving in the country's premier institutions.

America, as it faces the twenty-first century, is confronted with a major challenge in science and technology from European and Asian nations. At stake is the preservation of the United States as a world leader and superpower, jobs for our citizens, and the future standard of living for all Americans. The challenge must be met at all levels, from national to local, and the requisite changes that need to take place are nowhere more important than in the elementary and secondary schools.

Astronauts Guion Bluford, Ronald McNair, and Frederick Gregory

GEORGE WASHINGTON CARVER

One of the most well-known and distinguished of all African Americans, George Washington Carver is rightly considered among the most important scientists in American history. In 1896 Booker T. Washington hired Carver to teach at Tuskegee Institute in Alabama.

Around this same time Carver began raising the living standards of poor black farmers by teaching them to rotate crops, alternately planting sweet potatoes, corn, cowpeas, soybeans, peanuts, and cotton. As a professor at Tuskegee, Carver earned lasting fame for his development of more than 300 different uses for peanuts.

Carver received honorary doctorates and many important awards, including the Theodore Roosevelt Medal, honors from the Edison Foundation and London's Royal Society of Arts, and the National Association for the Advancement of Colored People (NAACP) Spingarn Medal. In 1936 Tuskegee Institute recognized Carver's fortieth year on the faculty by honoring him as the school's most productive teacher and researcher. Thirty years after his death, Carver was elected to the Hall of Fame for Great Americans. Congress has established January 5th as George Washington Carver Day.

Highlights in Medicine

The first trained black physician in the colonies was Lucas Santomee, who began his practice around 1667. Another early black American, Onesimus, introduced **inoculation** against smallpox to the colonies during the epidemic of 1721. But it would not be until 1876 that the first medical school established solely for blacks, Meharry Medical College in Nashville, Tennessee, was founded. Prior to that time, even free blacks had limited options for advanced medical study.

James McCune Smith was among those few fortunate enough to receive training from some of the best medical minds of the day, but he had to travel overseas to do so.

After excelling at the African Free School in New York City, Smith entered the University of Glasgow, Scotland. He then returned to New York and became a very successful physician, with a busy practice and two drug stores.

No doubt the greatest medical advancement for blacks—and for society as a whole—during the nineteenth century came at the hands of Daniel Hale Williams. In 1893 Williams performed the world's first successful heart operation. The surgery took place at Provident Hospital in Chicago, which Williams had founded just two years earlier. A patient was admitted to the emergency ward with a knife wound in an artery lying a fraction of an inch from the heart. With the aid of six staff surgeons, Williams

MAE C. JEMISON

The sky is no limit for Mae C. Jemison. The first African American woman selected to be an astronaut by the National Aeronautics and Space Administration (NASA), Jemison was aboard the space shuttle *Endeavor* when it lifted off for an eight-day mission on September 12, 1992.

Ever since she was a young girl Jemison was fascinated with science, especially astronomy, but her parents also stressed the importance of a well-rounded education. After graduating in 1977 from Stanford University with degrees in both chemical engineering and Afro-American studies, Jemison studied medicine at Cornell University. From 1983 to 1985 the young doctor joined the Peace Corps, an organization that works with the underprivileged in developing countries, and was stationed in West Africa.

After Jemison returned to the United States, she applied to NASA. One of 15 candidates selected from a field of nearly 2,000, she completed a gruelling year-long training and evaluation program to ready her for her duties aboard the *Endeavor.* A science specialist, on board she conducted life science experiments, including fertilizing frog eggs and seeing how they developed into tadpoles, and studied bone cell loss in an environment without gravity. She also helped the crew operate the shuttle and launch payloads and transport cargo and went on space walks.

Jemison resigned from NASA in 1993 to pursue her personal interests related to science education and minorities. In 1992 she visited a Detroit, Michigan, school named in her honor, the Mae C. Jemison Academy, and told the *Detroit Free Press* at the time that the dedication is "a privilege and a responsibility." In addition to her other pursuits, Jemison plans to return to the school to teach classes, conduct experiments, and help fuel students' interests in science.

Sources: Detroit Free Press, October 27, 1992; *Ebony,* October 1987, pp. 93-98.

made an incision, or cut, in the patient's chest and operated successfully on the artery. For the next four days the patient lay near death; ultimately, he recovered and Williams's fame spread (though many white doctors at first dismissed the possibility that a black man could perform so delicate and daring an operation).

Mae Jemison, physician and astronaut

Among twentieth-century highlights in black medicine are Charles Richard Drew's research in blood plasma, beginning in 1940; William A. Hinton's development of a test for detecting **syphilis;** Percy Lavon Julian's work with cortisone, a drug used to treat arthritis; and Samuel L. Kountz's advances in kidney transplantation.

For health issues related to African Americans, see Vol. 2, Ch. 15: "The Family and Health."

25
Sports

The African American
Amateur and Professional Athlete

FACT FOCUS

- In 1936, at the Berlin Olympic Games, Jesse Owens became the first Olympian ever to win four gold medals.
- Brooklyn Dodger second baseman Jackie Robinson broke the color barrier in baseball in 1947 and went on to be named rookie-of-the-year.
- High-jumper Alice Coachman became the first black woman to win an Olympic gold medal at the 1948 games in London.
- During the 1950s Althea Gibson became the first black to gain top honors in professional tennis.
- In 1958, after joining the Boston Bruins, Willie O'Ree became the first black hockey player in the National Hockey League.
- Hank Aaron, during a career that spanned three decades, hit more home runs (755) than anyone else in the history of major league baseball.
- By 1990 blacks comprised a full 60 percent of all NFL players. By 1992 blacks represented 75 percent of all NBA players. Today, 20 percent of baseball players are filled by African Americans and others of color.
- Of all sports, professional boxing has the best record for integration throughout its ranks.

"The majority of people in the world don't do what it takes to win. Everyone is looking for the easy road."—Charles Barkley

"The challenge is still there."—Wilma Rudolph

The untimely AIDS-related death of Arthur Ashe in 1993 robbed the black community of a pioneering sports hero who was also one of the most passionate and eloquent spokesmen for minority athletes.

Tennis great Arthur Ashe

Jesse Owens (center) accepts the gold medal at the 1936 Olympic games in Berlin, Germany

Ashe, the first black American man to win Wimbledon, the U.S. Open, and a Grand Slam of tennis, spent his entire career protesting unjust racial practices in the sporting world. Although richly talented and successful, Ashe was distressed by the discrimination he faced in his own career and by what he considered racist hiring and promotional tactics throughout collegiate and professional sports. As a tennis star, and later as an author and newspaper columnist, he called for equal opportunity in all aspects of athletics.

The concerns Ashe voiced have become critical issues as the $70 billion-a-year business of American sports moves toward the twenty-first century. The dilemma is obvious: though black players form the majority on the field in a number of professional and amateur sports, blacks are grossly underrepresented as owners, coaches, and managers.

Baseball

Before 1947 professional baseball was segregated and blacks played in the Negro leagues. These leagues provided the only opportunities for several generations of extremely talented and dedicated minority ballplayers. A surge in the popularity of baseball after World War II helped pave the way for black entry into the formerly all-white major leagues. Brooklyn Dodger second baseman Jackie Robinson broke the

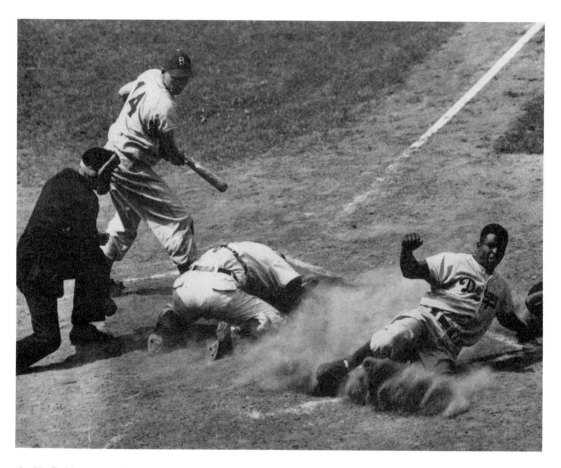

Jackie Robinson steals home

color barrier in 1947 and went on to be named rookie-of-the-year.

Robinson and other early black major leaguers faced second-class treatment in the Jim Crow South and widespread hostility from fans. Nevertheless, blacks began to stream into professional baseball, breaking records that had previously been held by white superstars. By the 1970s blacks were on the rosters of every team in the league and were increasingly joined by talented players from all parts of Latin America.

Today minority players—including those of color from the Caribbean and elsewhere—comprise some 20 percent of all major league positions.

A number of black athletes have risen to greatness in baseball. Hank Aaron holds the record for most career home runs. Ricky Henderson set a single-season record for stolen bases. Willie Mays is acclaimed as the game's greatest center fielder. Frank Robinson was the only player ever to win an most valuable player (MVP) award in both

Hank Aaron hit 755 home runs during his career in the majors

the National and American leagues and was the first black ever named manager of a major league **franchise.** And in 1993, two-time National League MVP Barry Bonds became the highest-paid baseball athlete of all time, with a contract that awarded him more than $7 million per year.

Interestingly, black participation in major league baseball peaked in the 1970s and has declined since. One factor sparking the change is the closing of inner-city baseball programs and urban Little Leagues due to lack of financial support. The economic situation has become so desperate in some American cities that even school athletic programs are threatened with cutbacks or termination.

Despite a declining black membership, major league baseball has made modest strides toward equal opportunity employment in the many franchise front offices. Frank Robinson became the first black manager in 1974, and since then a half-dozen other blacks have managed on the major league level. Bill White, a former All-Star, was named president of the National League in 1989. From his office on Park Avenue in New York City, White handles labor agreements, oversees league expansion, dispenses fines and suspensions, and enforces league rules. Teams employing blacks in high executive positions include the Baltimore Orioles, the Boston Red Sox, the Atlanta Braves, the Los Angeles Dodgers, and the Houston Astros.

Nevertheless, the percentage of black baseball managers, owners, and administrators lags far behind the percentage of black ballplayers. Jesse Jackson's Rainbow Commission for Fairness in Athletics has planned demonstrations outside major league ballparks and training facilities in order to remind both executives and fans that blacks—long superstars on the field—want to have a broader impact on the game.

Kareem Abdul-Jabbar

Basketball

Professional basketball began to integrate in 1951, when the Boston Celtics drafted Chuck Cooper and the New York Knicks hired Nat "Sweetwater" Clifton. By the late 1960s most of the sport's biggest stars were

minorities, including Bill Russell, Wilt Chamberlain, Kareem Abdul-Jabbar, Elvin Hayes, and Willis Reed. These and other talented athletes helped transform the game from a fairly polite and modest-paced game to a fast-breaking and highly physical contest.

Black players won more and more roster positions as the 1970s progressed. Such athletes as Abdul-Jabbar, Julius "Dr. J" Erving, Moses Malone, Bob McAdoo, and Wes Unseld helped further the evolution of the professional basketball game. By the 1980s black dominance of the sport was assured with the arrival of Earvin "Magic" Johnson, Patrick Ewing, Michael Jordan, Clyde Drexler, Charles Barkley, and Shaquille O'Neal.

A full three quarters of all National Basketball Association (NBA) players are

Earvin "Magic" Johnson

black. This reality was vividly reflected in the makeup of the first U.S. Olympic basketball team consisting of professional players. Of the 12 men asked to represent the nation at the 1992 Olympic Games, only two were white. The celebrated "Dream Team" won the gold medal easily.

Basketball was also one of the first major sports to hire black head coaches. Bill Russell was the first, in 1966. At one time as many as a half-dozen NBA head coaches were black. But by 1992 the number had declined to two. As many as 24 head coaches were hired and fired between 1990 and 1992—not one of them black. Disgruntled players have threatened a game-by-game boycott if more minority coaches are not hired by the end of this decade.

The situation in the NBA is not entirely hopeless, however. The Denver Nuggets are partially owned and fully run by African American businessman Bertram Lee. In addition, basketball was the only sport in 1992 to feature black general managers, with four in the position of representing the Los Angeles Clippers, the Denver Nuggets, the Cleveland Cavaliers, and the New Jersey Nets.

Of all sports, in fact, basketball seems to offer the brightest future for minority hiring. A generation of superstar players will soon retire with enough wealth to purchase controlling shares in franchises. This is a stated goal of Magic Johnson, who retired in 1992 after testing positive for the HIV virus and tried his hand at coaching the Los Angeles Lakers, and a possible goal of Michael Jordan as well, who retired in 1993 and later announced that he would attempt a second pro career in baseball.

Michael Jordan

For most people, the vast popularity of basketball in America eclipses any racial boundaries. The best players are not just African American heroes; they are American heroes. As such they have the power to shape public opinion, especially among the young. This power is displayed in everything from athletic shoe advertising to literacy programs and AIDS awareness, and it is likely to remain a vital force well into the twenty-first century.

Football

Unlike other major American sports, professional football began as an integrated entertainment. Blacks played alongside whites on the gridiron until 1930 after which, for 15 years, the sport was all-white. In 1945 a handful of black players were recruited, including Woodrow Strode of the Los Angeles Rams and Ben Willis of the Cleveland Browns.

During the 1950s the number of black players increased slowly. Then, in 1957, the history of the National Football League (NFL) was forever changed by the arrival of Jim Brown. Brown, a superstar for the Cleveland Indians, led the league in rushing for eight of his nine years in football and established a new career rushing record. By the time his tenure on the field came to an end in 1966, other black players had emerged as stars, among them Chicago Bears running back Gayle Sayers and New York Giants safety Emlen Tunnel.

One stumbling block remained for black football players: three key positions were quietly considered "white-only." These were middle linebacker, center, and quarterback. In the interests of winning games, however, these artificial boundaries eventually fell. Willie Lanier of the Kansas City Chiefs became the first in a long line of black All-Star middle linebackers. Quarterback James Harris of the Los Angeles Rams became the first black starter at his position in the 1970s. And centers Ray Donaldson of the Indianapolis Colts and Dwight Stephenson of the Miami Dolphins both turned in long careers as starters in the 1980s.

Black stars also redefined football's defensive game in the 1970s. The process began with the "Purple People Eaters" of the Minnesota Vikings defensive line—including Carl Eller, Allan Page, and Jim Marshal. It

Walter Payton

extended through the Los Angeles Rams' "Fearsome Foursome," which included Rosey Grier, David "Deacon" Jones, and Lamar Lundy. Possibly the best known unit, however, is the Pittsburgh Steelers' "Steel Curtain," including "Mean" Joe Greene, L. C. Greenwood, and Dwight White, who helped the Steelers win four Super Bowls.

An explosion of black talent characterized the 1980s. Chicago Bears running back Walter Payton did the unthinkable when he broke Brown's rushing record in 1984. Jerry Rice grabbed an all-time record 101 touchdown receptions and helped the San Francisco 49ers win two Super Bowls. Doug Williams overcame injuries to quarterback the underdog Washington Redskins to a Super Bowl victory in 1988. And two black starting quarterbacks, Warren Moon of the Houston Oilers and Randall Cunningham of the Philadelphia Eagles, shattered forever the myth that African Americans were unable to captain major league football teams.

The coaching ranks have been slow to integrate but are finally showing some progress. Art Shell of the Los Angeles Raiders became the first African American head coach of the modern era in 1990. And Dennis Green assumed the head coaching duties for the Minnesota Vikings in 1992. Professional football has also added three black coaches to the important positions of offensive and defensive coordinators. Executives in the NFL admit that the League must actively promote more black coaches. That promotion process should also change the low percentage of minority coaches at the college level, which has long been a source of frustration for talented blacks in football.

As with basketball, football players' salaries have risen dramatically since the mid-1980s, in part due to player-directed lawsuits and strikes. Front office personnel are more willing than ever to listen to and respond to star players' demands, a fact that may lead to profound changes in NFL management in the coming decades.

Boxing

Black athletes have been boxing professionally since colonial times. They have virtually dominated the sport since the 1930s, especially in the most popular heavyweight division. Joe Louis held the world heavyweight title for a record 11 years and eight months in the 1930s and 1940s, and the American public cheered for middleweight champion Sugar Ray Robinson when he demolished German opponent Max Schmeling prior to World War II. Henry Armstrong held three world titles at once—featherweight, lightweight, and welterweight—during the Great Depression.

Louis, Robinson, and Armstrong were stars in what is considered to be the first Golden Age of blacks in boxing. A new Golden Age dawned on March 8, 1971, when Muhammad Ali and Joe Frazier drew the sport's first multimillion-dollar gate. Ali, a national figure since winning an Olympic gold medal in 1960, was one of the first athletes to use his position to comment on American political and social events.

Joe Louis, 1936

Muhammad Ali

As purses for major boxing events approached $100 million per match in the mid-1980s due to pay-per-view television and cable network sponsorship, a new generation of fighters arose. "Iron" Mike Tyson, a tough youngster from Brooklyn, became the best-known heavyweight champion since Ali and the wealthiest boxer of all time. His **tumultuous** reign ended with a knockout by Buster Douglas, who in turn lost to Evander Holyfield. Holyfield was unseated in 1992 by Riddick Bowe, who came from the same Brooklyn projects as Tyson. Unlike the combative Tyson (who in 1992 began serving a six-year prison term for rape), Bowe earned a reputation for professionalism and social activism as he spoke against **apartheid** policies in South Africa,

Riddick Bowe

Almost singlehandedly he transformed boxing from a second-rank sport to a top-drawing entertainment.

No serious white contender has risen in boxing's heavyweight division since the days of Ali. Other divisions have also featured stellar black fighters. During the 1970s and 1980s fans were thrilled by middleweight and welterweight match-ups between Sugar Ray Leonard, Marvin Hagler, and Thomas Hearns. When Ali was no longer able to defend his heavyweight crown, new challengers such as Larry Holmes and Leon Spinks rose to the championship ranks.

Althea Gibson at Wimbeldon, 1957

Women in Sports

American sporting history has been greatly enriched by the activities of a number of talented black women athletes. From the championships won by tennis star Althea Gibson to the gold medals earned by Jackie Joyner-Kersee, women have garnered both fame and power through athletic endeavor.

High-jumper Alice Coachman became the first black woman to win an Olympic gold medal. She earned the gold at the 1948 Olympic Games in London, thus paving the way for generations of American athletes to come. Other Olympic medal-winners include Wilma Rudolph, who overcame a serious disability to snatch three gold medals in the 1960 Olympics; Florence Griffith Joyner,

and the need for more sports programs in the nation's ghettos. (A top boxer like Riddick Bowe can earn as much as $100 million for less than a dozen major ring events.)

Professional boxing features well-known black figures in all realms of the sport. Bowe, for instance, employs black trainers, including Eddie Futch, and a black manager, Rock Newman. Entrepreneur Don King is both the most famous and the wealthiest boxing promoter of the modern era. His powerful position in boxing's ranks—and his ability to court champion after champion—assure him continued success in his field.

Boxing is a brutal and dangerous sport demanding years of specialized training, **rigorous** conditioning, and single-minded dedication. The public appetite for major boxing events will continue to provide ample opportunities for talented athletes from all over the world.

Wilma Rudolph won the 1960 Olympic gold medals for the 100 meter run, 200 meter run, and 400 meter relay

551

Florence Griffith Joyner

One of the best-known black heroines in sports is Althea Gibson. During the crisis years of the civil rights era in the late 1950s, Gibson made her mark by winning a Grand Slam tennis tournament in 1956, two Wimbledon titles in 1957 and 1958, and the United States Lawn Tennis Association national singles championships in 1957 and 1958. Gibson was the first African American to gain top honors in professional tennis, and her performance paved the way for such stars as Arthur Ashe and Zina Garrison.

The increased political clout of women has brought about changes in attitudes toward competitive sports. While women may never achieve equality in spending for their athletic programs on college campuses and in public schools, a federal mandate has been issued to try to bridge the gap. The problem will become more crucial as a generation of women who have played competitive sports begin to produce children and encourage them to engage in athletics.

who captured three gold medals and one silver for track events at the 1988 Olympics; Debi Thomas, the first black woman to win an Olympic medal in figure skating with a bronze showing at the 1988 Olympics; and Jackie Joyner-Kersee, an Olympic champion in the grueling **heptathlon** competition and the long jump.

A 1992 *Sporting News* magazine list of the 100 most powerful Americans in sports included the name Anita DeFrantz. DeFrantz, who won a bronze medal for competitive rowing in the 1976 Olympics, is the first African American member of the International Olympic Committee. DeFrantz will play a crucial role in the planning of the 1996 Olympic Games in Atlanta, Georgia, and other international events as well.

Current Issues in Sports for African Americans

Minority Hiring

The 1990s have witnessed the flowering of a grass-roots movement to spark more minority hiring in all sports. From demonstrations led by Jesse Jackson to threats of player boycotts to assure more minority coaches, the message is becoming clear: equal opportunity employment must be extended to all areas of professional and amateur athletics, from the locker room to the boardroom.

The 1992 *Sporting News* magazine poll identifying the 100 most important people

Don King (center) with boxing champions Pinklon Thomas and Mike Tyson

in sports named only six blacks. Although 75 percent of the players in the NBA were black in 1992, only two head coaches were minorities. The same scenario held true for football. Sixty percent of the players in the NFL were black in 1992 but only two head coaches were black. Professional baseball has even seen a decline in the number of black players on the field. And some Professional Golf Association (PGA) golf tournaments are still held at private clubs with all-white memberships. Moreover, hockey, tennis, and horse racing have included only minimal numbers of blacks.

The situation is much the same at the amateur level. Black athletes have excelled at the Olympic Games, but a vast majority of college coaches, trainers, and athletic directors are white. Blacks are also scarce among the ranks of referees, umpires, play-by-play announcers, and agents.

Professional boxing has the best record for integration throughout its ranks. Many fighters—as well as trainers, managers, and promoters—are minorities. The flamboyant Don King, long a fixture in the sport, was one of the members of *The Sporting News*'s

Jackie Joyner-Kersee

list of the most important figures in organized athletics.

Black Spectators

Black attendance at sporting events has declined dramatically in recent years. In 1992 it was estimated that only 5 percent of paying customers for major league baseball were black. The glamorous arenas that serve as stages for athletic competition have been described by some as exclusive "country clubs" existing only to amuse the nation's wealthiest citizens. Many sports franchises

sponsor community outreach programs, but these do little to attract minority customers to the ball park.

Positive Developments

African Americans have made inroads into sports management, however. As president of baseball's National League, Bill White holds one of the sport's most influential positions. Professional basketball had four African American general managers in 1992: Elgin Baylor of the Los Angeles Clippers, Bernie Bickerstaff of the Denver

On April 1, 1989, Bill White became the first black president of Baseball's National League

Nuggets, Wayne Embry of the Cleveland Cavaliers, and Willis Reed of the New Jersey Nets. Art Shell of the Los Angeles Raiders and Dennis Green of the Minnesota Vikings are the first two black head coaches in professional football since 1923.

Track coach Bob Kersee had a taste of Olympic success when both his wife, Jackie Joyner-Kersee, and his sister-in-law, Florence Griffith Joyner, won Olympic medals. Agent W. Jerome Stanley negotiated a $16.5 million contract for Reggie Lewis of the Boston Celtics in 1990. Perhaps most important, Peter C. B. Bynoe and Bertram Lee became in 1989 the first African American managing partners of a major sports franchise—the Denver Nuggets of the NBA.

Today no one would dare argue, as baseball executive Al Campanis did in 1987, that blacks lack the "necessities" to manage or run sports teams. In fact, according to findings released by the Center for the Study of Sport and Society at Northeastern University, professional sports outstrips the wider American society in non-discriminatory hiring practices. A "report card" issued by the university gave society at large a "D" grade overall while the NBA averaged "B," the NFL, "B," and Major League Baseball, "C." The study took into consideration the vast number of black athletes and their salaries compared to those of their white teammates.

It is these athletes who stand poised to transform not only organized sports but society as well. Outside the entertainment industry, no other profession has supplied so many well-known and well-loved figures to the American public. No other industry could likely offer more opportunities for blacks to become role models, national heroes, or spokespersons for social causes. For instance, the discovery that Earvin "Magic" Johnson of the Los Angeles Lakers was infected with the AIDS virus did more to advance public knowledge of the disease than a decade of publicity had done.

Arthur Ashe was not prone to optimism about the future of African Americans in the business sector of sports, but he did hope for some improvement by the end of the decade. In an *Ebony* essay published in August of 1992, just a few months before his death, he wrote: "We as African-Americans will continue our cultural emphasis on sports participation, and we will make our mark in new areas." Ashe's words, like his life, should be inspiring for generations to come.

26

Military

African American
Servicemen and the Military Establishment

"The real story is that yes, I climbed, and I climbed well, and I climbed hard, and I climbed over the cliff, but always on the backs and the contributions of those who went before me."—Colin Powell

The experience of settling and defending America has been shared by people of many races and nationalities, including African Americans. Indeed, African Americans began serving America even before the nation was officially born and they have fought willingly and honorably in every major American conflict up to the present day. But as in other areas of American life, blacks in the military were long subject to discriminatory treatment and second-class status.

The American Revolution and the Revolutionary War (1775-83)

At the beginning of the Revolutionary War, blacks fought on equal ground with whites for a time, but by the end of 1775 black enlistment was made all but impossible by Southern Congressmen. This would change three years later when victory over

the British became more important than caving in to the fears and demands of slave-owners.

One of the key events that brought about the war was a clash between the Americans and the British in 1770 called the Boston Massacre. Escaped slave Crispus Attucks died in the clash, along with four other Americans. (The state of Massachusetts later honored Attucks with a statue in Boston.)

During the war blacks served in a variety of posts—as spies, pilots, and infantrymen, as well as laborers, cooks, and teamsters. Some blacks were with the Minutemen at Lexington and Concord; others wintered with George Washington at Valley Forge, crossing the Delaware with him en route to a surprise attack against the Hessians, who were quartered at Trenton. Two blacks, Peter Salem and Salem Poor, were singled out for bravery after the Battle of Bunker Hill in 1775.

By 1778 the Continental Army was racially integrated: on average, each brigade contained 42 black soldiers. All told, between 8,000 and 10,000 blacks served in the armies of the Revolutionary War. And many more served in the Revolutionary Navy. Yet despite their valor and dedication, and their major role in the fight for American independence, blacks were excluded from the military beginning in 1792.

The War of 1812

The War of 1812 was mainly fought by naval forces, and black sailors made up approximately 20 percent of Navy crews. While the Army and Marine Corps continued to exclude blacks, the Louisiana legislature authorized enlistments of free black landowners in the militia. The combat bravery of black troops was a key factor in the American victory at the Battle of New Orleans, though it was fought after the war had officially ended.

The Civil War (1861-65)

At the outbreak of the Civil War, the United States suffered a near-fatal blow. Led

---

1777 Vermont becomes the first state to ban slavery and the Connecticut legislature grants equal pay for white and black soldiers.

1792 Congress restricts military service to white males.

1864 The Army **Appropriations** Act approves identical pay for black and white soldiers.

1917 An all-black Officer Training School is established at Fort Dodge; however, the War Department has an iron-clad rule: No black officer can command white officers or enlisted men.

1940 Benjamin O. Davis, Sr., becomes the nation's first African American general.

1979 Hazel Johnson becomes the first African American woman general and is placed in command of the Army Nurse Corps.

1985 Sherian Grace Cadoria becomes the first black woman to obtain the rank of brigadier general in the regular army.

1989 Colin L. Powell becomes the first black chairman of the Joint Chiefs of Staff.

A rifle company of black Union soldiers

by Robert E. Lee, nearly half of the West Point-trained U.S. Army officer corps **defected** to the Confederacy. Lacking a reservoir of trained military leaders, the nation had to recruit, train, and deploy an expanded military. One result was the passing of a law requiring more funding and education in military science, a program that later became known as the Reserve Officers' Training Corps (ROTC).

As soon as the war began, blacks outside of the rebel territory volunteered for the Army. Expecting a short war, the secretary of war rejected their offers. Although some Army leaders such as Major General John C. Frémont sought to recruit blacks as soldiers, the Lincoln administration canceled such actions.

Meanwhile, the Confederacy enjoyed the fruits of slave labor in constructing forts and related combat service support roles. By 1862, after important military setbacks, Congress lifted the ban on blacks and approved their use as Union Army laborers. This same year Robert Smalls of South Carolina became one of the war's first black heroes. A member of a crew in the Confederate Navy, Smalls sailed a Confederate steamer named the *Planter* out of Charleston and turned it over to the Union. Smalls then joined the Union Navy (and distinguished himself after the war as a five-term U.S. Congressman).

United States Colored Troops (USCT)

Following the Emancipation Proclama-

Troop E of the 9th U.S. Cavalry (the Buffalo Soldiers), 1895

tion in September 1862, Massachusetts was permitted to organize the black 54th and 55th Massachusetts Infantry regiments. (The exploits of the 54th Massachusetts, one of the most celebrated black units in history, inspired the motion picture *Glory.*) In May 1863 the severe manpower shortage forced the War Department to approve organization of black regiments with all-white officers. The units were designated as United States Colored Troops (USCT).

Thereafter, blacks fought and died in every major Civil War action. For a time, they served for less pay than white troops.

But in some units, black troops refused to accept the lesser pay. After strong protests by both black and white citizens, the 1864 Army **Appropriations** Act approved a uniform pay scale for all soldiers.

The Medal of Honor

This nation's highest decoration for valor was established on December 21, 1861. Issuance was initially limited to enlisted men of the Navy and Marine Corps, but the award was expanded to include the Army on July 12, 1862. On March 3, 1863, commissioned officers also became eligible for the

Medal of Honor. During the Civil War, 1,523 Medals of Honor were awarded, 23 of which went to black servicemen. The first black recipient was Sergeant William H. Carney, 54th Massachusetts Infantry, for combat valor on July 18, 1863, at Fort Wagner, South Carolina.

By the end of the Civil War some 38,000 black troops had died—around 35 percent of all blacks who served in combat. United States Colored Troops made up 13 percent of the Union Army.

The Indian Campaigns (1866-90)

Following the Civil War America acquired a new appreciation of the importance of military power. In 1866 the 39th Congress passed legislation to "increase and fix the Military Establishment of the United States." The peacetime army would have five artillery regiments, ten cavalry regiments, and forty-five infantry regiments. This legislation also declared "That to the six regiments of cavalry now in service shall be added four regiments, two of which shall be composed of colored men."

With that new law, the nation gained its first all-black Regular Army regiments: The 9th and 10th Cavalry, and the 24th and 25th Infantry—the "Buffalo Soldiers." Although the term "Buffalo Soldiers" initially referred to these four post-Civil War regiments, it has been adopted with pride by veterans of all racially segregated black Army ground units of the 1866-1950 era.

Surprisingly—given portrayals of the Old West in movies and elsewhere—approximately 20 percent of Army soldiers on duty in the West were black. According

Former Buffalo Solider Alpheus Jones in his old cavalry uniform next to a poster for a new U.S. postage stamp commemorating the soliders, 1994

to historian Gary Donaldson in the 1991 book *The History of African-Americans in the Military,* "even today, few Americans realize that when the cavalry came to the rescue of white settlers in the Old West that the rescuers, those gallant soldiers in blue, might well have been black" (Fort Krieger Publishing Co.). The heroism of black soldiers is underscored by the 18 Medals of Honor they earned during what historians term both "The Indian Campaigns" and "The Plains War."

Black participation in the war against Native Americans was full of historical ironies; while fighting another race repressed by whites, black soldiers fought antiblack attitudes within the U.S. military itself.

One of many painful episodes for the original Buffalo Soldiers was the case of Second Lieutenant Henry Ossian Flipper. Born in Thomasville, Georgia, on March 21, 1856, Flipper was the first black to graduate from the U.S. Military Academy at West Point, New York. He ranked fiftieth among the 76 members of the Class of 1887, and became the only black commissioned officer in the Regular Army. Assigned initially to Fort Sill, Oklahoma Territory, Flipper was eventually sent to Fort Davis, Texas. There he assumed the routine duties of a newly commissioned officer, such as surveying and supervising construction projects. Flipper also acquired some combat experience fighting Apache Indians led by Chief Victoria.

In August 1881 Lieutenant Flipper was arrested and charged with failing to mail $3,700 in checks to the Army Chief of Commissary. The young lieutenant was then tried by court-martial for theft and conduct unbecoming an officer. He was cleared of the first charge (the checks were found in his quarters), but convicted of the second. Upon confirmation of his sentence by President Chester Arthur, Flipper was dismissed from the service on June 30, 1882. Returning to civilian life, working for mining companies, Flipper used his West Point education as a surveyor and engineer. He also published his memoirs as well as technical books dealing with both Mexican and Venezuelan laws.

Nearly a century after Flipper left West Point, a review of his record indicated that he had been framed by his fellow officers.

His records were corrected and he was granted an honorable discharge from the Army. On the one-hundredth anniversary of his graduation, his bust was unveiled and is now displayed in the Cadet Library at the Military Academy.

There were only two other nineteenth-century black graduates of West Point: John H. Alexander (1864-1894) in the Class of 1887; and Charles A. Young (1864-1922) in the Class of 1889. After Young's graduation, it would take 47 years for another black cadet to graduate from West Point.

The Spanish-American War (1898)

America's "Ten Week War" with Spain marked the nation's emergence as a global colonial power. Although the United States had just completed its own "Indian Campaigns," the tension between the two nations arose from Spain's treatment of Cuba's native population, who increasingly resisted harsh Spanish rule on the island. In 1885 open rebellion by the Cuban people resulted in a brutal response by the Spanish. The battleship U.S.S. *Maine* was sent to Cuba to protect U.S. interests there and to serve as a clear reminder of America's intention to enforce the **Monroe Doctrine.**

On the evening of February 15, 1898, a gigantic explosion rocked the warship. It sank rapidly in Havana harbor, killing 266 U.S. Navy sailors—22 of them black Americans. Although the cause of the *Maine*'s sinking was undetermined, the disaster inflamed Americans, who adopted the slogan, "Remember the *Maine,* to hell with Spain."

On March 29, the United States issued an **ultimatum** to Spain, demanding the release of Cubans from brutal detention camps, the declaration of an armistice, and preparations for peace negotiations. The Spanish government did not comply, and on April 19, proclaiming Cuba free and independent, Congress authorized the President to use U.S. troops to remove Spanish forces from Cuba.

The Spanish-American War was especially important for African Americans because it was the first time black men served in every Army grade below general officer. The Regular Army of only 28,000 men included the all-black 9th and 10th Calvary regiments, and the 24th and 25th Infantry regiments. All four regiments distinguished themselves during combat in Cuba. An expansion force of 175,000 troops came from the Federalized state militia/national guard reservoir, designated United States Volunteer Infantry (USVI).

The USVI included the nation's oldest all-black national guard unit, originally formed in Chicago and known as the Hannibal Guards. The unit was renamed the 9th Battalion on May 5, 1890, and was commanded by an African American, Major Benjamin G. Johnson. When the war erupted, other all-black militia regiments were organized, including the 3rd Alabama, the 23th Kansas, the 3rd North Carolina, the 9th Ohio, the 6th Virginia, and the 8th Illinois. Until converted to artillery battalions in World War II, the 8th Illinois was always commanded by a black officer.

Although only ten weeks long, the Spanish-American War produced six black Medal of Honor recipients, with five from the 10th Cavalry, which fought as infantry in Cuba. A black sailor won the sixth medal for heroism aboard the U.S.S. *Iowa* in the waters off Santiago, Cuba.

The Spanish-American War provided a small increase in the number of black Regular Army Officers. Benjamin O. Davis, Sr., served as a lieutenant in the 8th Illinois USVI. Having been discharged, he enlisted on June 14, 1899, as a private in the 9th Cavalry; he was promoted to corporal, and then to sergeant major. Davis was commissioned a Regular Army second lieutenant of cavalry on February 2, 1901. In 1940 Davis would become the nation's first black general officer (see below, "World War II"). Also commissioned as Regular Army officers in 1901 were John R. Lynch and John E. Green. As the twentieth century began, the United States Army had four black commissioned officers.

World War I

The nation's entry into World War I again raised the question of how to utilize black troops. Of the more than 400,000 black soldiers who served during the war, only about 10 percent were assigned to combat duty in two infantry divisions. The 92nd Infantry Division was composed mainly of draftees. Black men from the 8th Infantry of the Illinois National Guard and the 315th Infantry of the New York National Guard formed the 93rd Infantry Division (Provisional). The majority of black World War I soldiers were assigned to dock-managing units at ports or labor units as quartermaster troops.

The most difficult issue facing the War Department was the demand that blacks be trained as commissioned officers. Initially, the idea was dismissed as laughable: It was considered to be "common knowledge" that

Navy sailors

black men inherently lacked leadership qualities. Only the resolve of the National Association for the Advancement of Colored People (NAACP), the Urban League, and such black newspapers as the *Chicago Defender* changed War Department policy. An all-black Officer Training School was established at Fort Dodge, near Des Moines, Iowa. On October 14, 1917, the school graduated and commissioned 639 black officers. However, the War Department had an iron-clad rule: No black officer could command white officers or enlisted men.

One solution to the issue of utilizing black officers and soldiers was characteristic of military racism of the time: Several black regi-

ments were "attached" to the allied French Army. Colonel William Hayward, commander of New York's 369th Infantry, criticized General John J. Pershing for this decision. Hayward, according to Arthur W. Little in the 1936 book *From Harlem to the Rhine: The Story of New York's Colored Volunteers,* charged that Pershing "simply put the black orphan in a basket, set it on the doorstep of the French, pulled the bell, and went away."

Despite the imposed "orphan" status, it was the 369th Infantry Regiment (15th New York) that established the best World War I record of any United States Army infantry regiment. The 369th served for 191 consecutive days in the trenches and never lost a foot

Members of the 369th Infantry, World War I

of ground to the Germans. The so-called "Harlem Hell Fighters" won their laurels attached to the French 4th Army, using French weapons and wearing U.S. uniforms.

In 1919 Columbia University President Nicholas Murray Butler gave *Harper's Weekly* his opinion of the 369th Infantry Regiment: "No American soldier saw harder or more constant fighting and none gave better accounts of themselves. When fighting was to be done, this regiment was there."

Despite the Jim Crow atmosphere, black soldiers earned an impressive number of awards for combat bravery defeating German troops. Sergeant Henry Johnson of New York's 369th Infantry Regiment was the first American, black or white, to receive the French Croix de Guerre (Cross of War). France awarded its Croix de Guerre to 34 black officers and 89 black enlisted men during the war. In the 92nd Division, 14 black officers and 34 black enlisted men earned the United States Army Distinguished Flying Cross (DFC). Ten officers and 34 enlisted men of the 93rd Division were DFC recipients.

Posthumous Medal of Honor Awarded

No Medal of Honor was awarded to a black serviceman during World War I. But in 1988 the Department of the Army researched the National Archives to determine whether racial barriers had prevented award of the nation's highest decoration for valor.

The archives search produced evidence that Corporal Freddie Stowers of Anderson County, South Carolina, had been recommended for the award; for "unknown reasons," however, the recommendation had not been processed. Stowers was a squad leader in Company C, 371st Infantry Regiment, 93rd Division. On September 28, 1918, he led his squad through heavy machine gun fire and destroyed the gun position on Hill 188 in the Champagne Marne Sector, France. Mortally wounded, Stowers continued to lead his men through a second trench line.

On April 24, 1991, President George Bush belatedly presented Stowers's Medal of Honor to his surviving sisters in a White House ceremony.

The Interwar Years (1919-40)

With the end of the war, the nation generally returned to the racial theory of "separate but equal." Some senior white Army officers supported barring enlistment or reenlistment of blacks altogether, an action that would have eventually abolished the nation's four black Regular Army regiments.

Much of the Army's antiblack sentiment was directed against black commissioned officer. Despite countless well-documented cases of superb combat leadership, most black officers were eliminated from active duty following World War I.

Those who argued against keeping black officers accused them of poor performance and criticized the black Officer Training School (OTS) class at Des Moines, Iowa. One of the severest critics was Major General Charles C. Ballou, commander of the World War I 93rd Infantry Division.

However, there were combat-experienced white officers who held a very different view of black officer training, such as Major Thomas A. Roberts. "As I understand the question," Roberts wrote in a letter dated April 5, 1920, "what the progressive Negro desires today is the removal of discrimination against him; that this can be accomplished in a military sense I believe to be largely possible, but not if men of the two races are segregated."

As for commissioned officers, the ROTC detachments at Howard and Wilberforce Universities provided the bulk of new black second lieutenants. With no funds for black officers to attend service schools, the lack of opportunity caused a considerable drop in the number of black reserve officers. To retain their commissions, other officers took advantage of correspondence and specially organized lecture/seminar courses.

World War II

Less than two months after war began in Europe, the nation's leading black organizations, the NAACP and the Urban League, had mobilized to defeat American racial segregation as well as Axis **fascism.** The black community clearly foresaw that the United States would eventually ally itself with Britain and France in war against Germany, Italy, and Japan.

Military mobilization began on August 27, 1940, with the federalizing of the National Guard and activation of the Organized Reserve. When Japan attacked Pearl Harbor on December 7, 1941, there were 120,000 officers and 1,523,000 enlisted men on active duty in the Army and its Air Corps. On September 16, 1940, the nation began its first peacetime draft. By the end of World War II, the Selective Service System had enlisted 10,110,104 men; 1,082,539 (10.7 percent) were black.

America's war effort required rapid expansion of both military and industrial power. Victory depended on the constant provision of ammunition, guns, planes, tanks, naval vessels, and merchant ships. The nation would have to unite to survive. A minority number of blacks, including Nation of Islam founder Elijah Muhammad, openly favored a Japanese victory; Muhammad's stance led to a four-year term in the U.S. Penitentiary at Milan, Michigan.

Essential to the work of both the NAACP and the Urban League was the impact of black-owned weekly newspapers such as Robert S. Abbott's *Chicago Defender* and Robert Vann's *Pittsburgh Courier.* The rallying slogan was the "Double V"—victory against fascism abroad and racial discrimination at home—and equal opportunity in both the armed services and within the civilian defense industries was the goal.

Soon, the NAACP and the Urban League were joined by the black activists of the March on Washington movement led by A. Philip Randolph of the Brotherhood of Sleeping Car Porters and Maids. Randolph predicted that upwards of 100,000 blacks would march on Washington, D.C., demanding equal employment opportunities in defense plant employment. On June 25, 1941, a week before the scheduled march, President Franklin D. Roosevelt averted the march by issuing Executive Order 8802. The order established a Committee on Fair Employment Practice "to provide for the full and equitable participation of all workers in defense industries, without discrimination." However, the order did not apply to the armed services.

The necessity of winning the war opened the economy to millions of black men and women who surged into defense plants, earning the same wages as their white coworkers. The war years thus brought economic upward mobility for many black civilians. Through the postwar benefits of the G.I. Bill of Rights, furthermore, the number of black college graduates and home owners would increase dramatically.

The public has largely ignored the fact that the United States Army first took steps toward racial integration early in World War II. The obvious waste of extra facilities caused the Army to operate all of its 24 Officer Candidate Schools as racially integrated institutions. Those who survived the standard three-month course were commissioned as second lieutenants in one of the 24 Army branches, ranging from the Army Air Forces Administrative School (Miami, Florida) to the Tank Destroyer School (Camp Hood, Texas). Upon graduation, black officers were assigned only to black units.

The Army Air Force (AAF)

The Army Air Force Aviation Cadet program that trained pilots, bombardiers, and navigators was an exception among racially integrated Army officer programs. Ironically, black non-flying officers graduated from the integrated AAF Officer Candidates School at Miami Beach.

A total of 926 black pilots earned their commissions and wings at the segregated Tuskegee Army Air Field (TAAF) near Chehaw, Alabama. The 673 single-engine TAAF pilot graduates would eventually form the four squadrons of the 332nd Fighter Group.

Led by Lieutenant Colonel Benjamin O. Davis, Sr., a 1936 West Point graduate, the 99th Fighter Squadron was assigned to the 33rd Fighter Group commanded by Colonel William M. Momeyer. The 99th's first mission was a June 2, 1943, strafing attack on the Italian island of Pantelleria. On this date, Captain Charles B. Hall scored the squadron's first air victory by shooting down an FW-190 and damaging an ME-109. The 99th then settled into normal operations, or so the men thought.

In September Davis was recalled to take command of the 332nd Fighter Group. That is when he and the black community discovered that the "Tuskegee Experiment" was about to be labeled a failure. Colonel Meyer's appraisal of the 99th Fighter Squadron was extremely negative:

> Based on the performance of the 99th Fighter Squadron to date, it is my opinion that they are not of the fighting caliber of any squadron in this group. They have failed to display the aggres-

Benjamin O. Davis, Sr.

> siveness and daring for combat that are necessary to a first class fighting organization. It may be expected that we will get less work and less operational time out of the 99th Fighter Squadron than any squadron in this group.

On October 16, 1943, squadron commander Davis appeared before the War Department's Committee on Special [Negro] Troop Policies to answer his group commander's allegations.

In his 1991 autobiography, written after his retirement as an Air Force lieutenant general, Davis describes the 1943 hearing:

> It would have been hopeless for me to stress the hostility and racism of whites as the motive behind the letter,

although that was clearly the case. Instead, I had to adopt a quiet, reasoned approach, presenting the facts about the 99th in a way that would appeal to fairness and win out over ignorance and racism.

Davis presented such a convincing case that Army Chief of Staff General George C. Marshall ordered a G-3 [operations] study of the black squadron, which revealed the 99th compared favorably to the other Fighter Squadrons.

On October 13, 1942, the Army had activated the 100th, 301st, and 302nd Fighter Squadrons. Combined with the 99th, the four squadrons would become the 332nd Fighter Group. Colonel Robert R. Selway, Jr., a white pilot, was its initial commanding officer. But with the 99th validated by the G-3 study, Davis assumed command of the Fighter Group at Selfridge Army Air Field in Michigan.

The 332nd departed for Italy on January 3, 1944, and absorbed the 99th as its fourth squadron. It became famous as a flying escort for heavy bombers and was the only AAF fighter group that never lost an escorted bomber to enemy planes. The 332nd Fighter Group had an impressive wartime record, having destroyed 103 enemy aircraft during 1,578 combat missions. In addition to more than 100 Distinguished Flying Crosses, the 332nd also earned three Distinguished Unit Citations.

The so-called "Tuskegee Experiment" thus proved that black men could fly state-of-the-art aircraft, and could also conduct highly successful combat operations meeting AAF standards. The fruit of the Tuskegee Airmen's efforts would be harvested in less than three years, when the United States military desegregated in 1948.

The Ground War

The World War II U.S. Army fielded two major black combat organizations: The 92nd Infantry Division in Europe, and the 93rd Infantry Division in the Pacific.

Just as in World War I, the 93rd Division was employed only in a fragmented manner. It spent most of its time island-hopping, relieving units that had defeated Japanese troops. The 93rd Division World War II casualties included 12 killed in action; 121 wounded in action; and 5 who died of wounds. Generally, the division's performance was considered to be adequate. Although white officers made the usual after-action comments concerning the lack of initiative among the 93rd's junior officers, the division was generally described as well-disciplined and having good morale.

The 92nd: A Valuable and Painful Lesson

The 92nd, in contrast, gained a reputation as a chaotic outfit. During its preparation for deployment overseas, elements of the 92nd Division were sprinkled across the United States. While the division headquarters were at Fort Huachuca, Arizona, subordinate units were stationed at Fort McClellan, Alabama; Camp Robinson, Arkansas; Camp Breckinridge, Kentucky; and Camp Atterbury, Indiana. The division's World War II casualty figures were vastly different than those of the 93rd Division: 548 killed in action; 2,187 wounded in action; and 68 who died of wounds. From its training in the

The 92nd Infantry Division, in the Ponsacco area of Italy, 1944

United States through combat in Europe, the division's main problem seemed to be its commander, Major General Edward M. Almond. Many veterans of the 92nd Division continue to blame Almond for the division's reputation and casualties.

It appears that "Ned" Almond was no closet racist. In a 1984 interview retired Lieutenant General William P. Ennis, Jr. gave a "warts and all" description of Almond. As a World War II brigadier general, Ennis had commanded the corps artillery that supported the 92nd Division. According to Ennis, Almond and many white Southern officers in the division were selected because "in theory, they knew more about handling Negroes than anybody else, though I can't imagine why because [Almond] just despised the ground they walked on" (quoted in Dale E. Wilson, "Recipe for Failure: Major General Edward M. Almond and

Preparation of the United States 92nd Infantry Division for Combat in World War II," *The Journal of Military History*, 1992).

The contrast of attitude at the division's various posts was amazing. While Almond **denigrated** the competence of black officers, Officer Candidate School (OCS) commandants were generally of the opposite opinion.

Almond established his headquarters at Viareggio, Italy, on October 5, 1944. Two days later, the division's 370th Infantry Regiment began its assault on Massa. Military historian Ulysses Lee, in his 1966 work *The Employment of Negro Troops,* described the 92nd Division's major weakness:

It was a problem in faith and lack of it—the wavering faith of commanders in the ability and determination of subordinates and enlisted men, and the continuation in the minds of enlisted men of training period convictions that they could not trust their leaders.

Thus, the Massa attack quickly turned into chaos. In what was to be a major charge against the division, the men began to "melt away" from the fighting. After Massa, there were increasing cases of mutinous behavior toward both black and white officers.

In February 1945 the 92nd became the focus of a Pentagon inquiry. The man who would examine the situation was Truman K. Gibson, Jr., a black insurance company lawyer from Chicago, and Civilian Aide to Secretary of War Henry L. Stimpson. In his assessment, Gibson refused to blame the victim, or to generalize about the capabilities of black soldiers based on the performance of Almond's 92nd Division. In a March 14 news conference in Rome, Gibson maintained that "If the division proves anything, it does not prove that Negroes can't fight. There is no question in my mind about the courage of Negro officers or soldiers and any generalization on the basis of race is entirely unfounded."

On May 14, 1945, a week after Germany surrendered, Lieutenant Colonel Marcus H. Ray wrote a letter to Gibson. A Chicagoan, as was Gibson, Ray was a National Guard officer of the 8th Illinois when it was mobilized in 1940. He ended the war as commanding officer of the 600th Field Artillery Battalion of the 92nd Division. Colonel Ray closed his letter to Gibson by observing:

Those who died in the proper performance of their assigned duties are our men of the decade and all honor should be paid them. They were Americans before all else. Racially, we have been the victims of an unfortunate chain of circumstances backgrounded by the unchanged American attitude as regards the proper "place" of the Negro.... I do not believe the 92nd a complete failure as a combat unit, but when I think of what it might have been, I am heart-sick.

The 761st Tank Battalion

The most highly acclaimed black ground combat unit of World War II was the 761st Tank Battalion. As an organization, it enjoyed the opposite circumstances of the 92nd Division. Before the United States entered World War II, some white Army officers favored opening opportunities for black soldiers. They rejected the view of fellow officers that modern weaponry was "too technical" for blacks. Fortunately, one such officer became the Commanding General of Army Ground Forces.

In this post, Lieutenant General Lesley James McNair spent most of his time visiting the nationwide array of ground forces training camps. And when he visited the 761st at Camp Claiborne, Louisiana, he openly praised and encouraged the Army's first black tankers. When the 761st went ashore in France on October 10, 1944, the men believed that their outfit's existence was due mainly to McNair. (General McNair was killed by United States "friendly fire" on July 25, 1944 in France. The Joint Chiefs of Staff National Defense University is located at Fort Lesley J. McNair, named in his honor, in Washington, D.C.).

When the 761st joined the 26th Division on October 31, the division commander, Major General Willard S. Paul, welcomed them, saying: "I am damned glad to have you with us. We have been expecting you for a long time, and I am sure you are going to give a good account of yourselves." Two days later, General George S. Patton visited and welcomed the 761st.

The 761st initial combat was on November 8, 1944 at Athaniville, France—the first of 183 continuous days of combat for the battalion. During their advance through six European countries, the 761st proved to be a superior combat organization.

The battalion is credited with killing 6,266 enemy soldiers and capturing 15,818. Despite its outstanding combat record, the 761st did not receive a well-deserved Presidential Unit Citation until January 24, 1978.

The veterans of the 761st still pursue a World War II mission: a **posthumous** Medal of Honor for Staff Sergeant Ruben Rivers, of Tecumseh, Oklahoma. Rivers was severely wounded on November 16, 1944, when his tank ran over two mines near Guebling, France. With his lower thigh torn and his knee bone protruding, Rivers refused evacuation. Instead, he remained with his tank and crew for three days of continuous combat. When his company was taken under fire by German heavy weapons, the company commander ordered his tanks to pull back below the crest of a hill. Rivers's tank opened fire at the enemy and continued firing until it was hit in the turret by an armor-piercing round that killed Rivers.

The Sea Services

In 1932—after a decade of having excluded blacks from enlisting—the United States Navy decided to award them their own branch. The black community referred to the branch—called the Steward's Service—as "sea-going bell hops." The 1940 Navy consisted of 170,000 men, of whom 4,007 were blacks in the Stewards' Service. In addition to blacks, Navy stewards also were recruited from among Filipino and other Asian American populations.

The advent of World War II transformed this situation. President Franklin D. Roosevelt had served as assistant secretary of the Navy during World War I and considered it "his branch" of the armed services. Therefore his January 9, 1942, memo to the Navy had tremendous impact. The President noted to then-Secretary of the Navy Frank Knox: "I think that with all the Navy activities, Bureau of Navy might invent something that colored enlistees could do in addition to the rating of messman."

The Navy did relent on April 7, 1942, by announcing it would accept 14,000 black enlistees in all ratings and branches. The initial training of black sailors was conducted at the Great Lakes Naval Training Station, north of Chicago, Illinois.

It was at Great Lakes that the Navy finally made a breakthrough in regard to black personnel. In January 1944, 16 black petty officers began a special intensive course of instruction that was conducted without public announcement. Three months later the Navy announced the commissioning of 12 black ensigns and 1 warrant officer. They were then and are now the Navy's "Golden Thirteen."

Shortly after the "Golden Thirteen" were commissioned, the Navy opened the V-12 officer training programs to black men. Among the V-12 graduates who became Navy officers in World War II were Samuel R. Gravely and Carl T. Rowan. Gravely became the Navy's first black admiral; Rowan returned to civilian life and became a syndicated columnist and broadcaster.

By the end of World War II, 165,000 blacks had served in the Navy; 17,000 in the Marine Corps; 5,000 in the Coast Guard; 12,000 in Construction Battalions (Sea Bees); and 24,000 in the Merchant Marine.

These African American soldiers served with distinction. Notable among them is the mess steward Dorie Miller, who on December 7, 1941 manned a machine gun aboard the U.S.S. *Arizona* as Japanese aircraft attacked Pearl Harbor. Miller destroyed two of the attackers and, after some delay, was awarded the Navy Cross. He was also pro-

Admiral Chester Nimitz awards Dorie Miller with the Navy Cross

moted to mess attendant first class. Miller died when the escort aircraft carrier U.S.S. *Liscome Bay* was sunk on November 24, 1943. Three other black mess attendants received the Navy Cross during World War II: Eli Benjamin (U.S.S. *Intrepid*); Leonard Harmon (U.S.S. *San Francisco*); and William Pinkney (U.S.S. *Enterprise*). Dorie Miller is memorialized by one of the three Navy warships named for black Americans, the U.S.S. *Miller*; the other two are the U.S.S. *Jesse L. Brown* and the U.S.S. *George Washington Carver.*

The Move Toward Equality in the Ranks

As the Allied victory of World War II approached, the highest levels of the United States government recognized that a new

2nd Infantry Division, Korea, 1950

racial era had emerged. Following the war the demand for desegregation of the military became a key political issue in black America. By May 1948, as that year's presidential election intensified, President Harry S Truman decided to desegregate the armed forces by Executive Order No. 9981—a policy for which blacks had lobbied—thereby ensuring Truman strong black support at the polls.

The Korean War

As North Korean forces surged across the 38th parallel on June 25, 1950, only the Air Force had desegregated. The United States ground forces in Korea were savaged by the North Koreans and driven south.

The first U.S. victory of the Korean War was won by black soldiers of the 24th Infantry Regiment on July 20, 1950, at Yechon. Captain Charles M. Bussey, a World War II Tuskegee Airman, was the ground commander and earned a Silver Star at Yechon. Two black soldiers were awarded posthumous Medals of Honor during the Korean War: Private First Class (PFC) William Thompson and Sergeant Cornelius H. Charlton, both of the 24th Infantry Regiment.

Thompson distinguished himself by

bravery and determination above and beyond the call of duty in action against the enemy on August 6, 1950, near Haman, Korea. While his platoon was reorganizing under cover of darkness, enemy forces overwhelmed the unit with a surprise attack. Johnson set up his machine gun in the path of the onslaught and swept the enemy with fire, momentarily pinning them down and thus permitting the remainder of his platoon to withdraw to a more secure position. Although hit repeatedly by grenade fragments and small-arms fire, he resisted his comrades' advice to withdraw. Steadfast at his machine-gun, he continued to deliver fire until he was mortally wounded by an enemy grenade.

Charlton, a member of Company C, distinguished himself in action against the enemy on June 2, 1951, near Chipo-Ri, Korea. His platoon was attacking heavily defended hostile positions on commanding ground when the leader was wounded and evacuated. Charlton assumed command, rallied the men, and spearheaded the assault against the hill. Personally eliminating two hostile positions and killing six of the enemy with his rifle-fire and grenades, he continued up the slope until the unit suffered heavy casualties and was stalled. Regrouping the men, he led them forward, only to be again forced back by a shower of grenades. Despite a severe chest wound, Charlton refused medical attention and led a third daring charge that would advance to the crest of the ridge. He then charged a remaining enemy position on a nearby slope alone and, though hit again by a grenade, raked the position with fire that eliminated it and routed the defenders. He died of wounds he received during his daring exploits.

By the end of the Korean War, racial segregation had been removed from most areas of the United States armed services. In the years preceding the Vietnam War, blacks increasingly entered the services and opted for full careers. Between 1953 and 1961 there was a slow but steady increase in the number of black career officers in each service.

Vietnam

During the brief period of cease-fire between the end of the Korean War and the heightening of conflict in Vietnam, the Kennedy Administration—prompted by Congressman Adam Clayton Powell, Jr., and others—sought to end any remaining discrimination in the Armed Forces. Through Secretary of Defense Robert McNamara, Kennedy stressed to military leaders the need for fostering friendship and equal opportunity for black servicemen, both on and off base.

By 1965 the United States had committed combat troops to Vietnam to support both the South Vietnamese people and U.S. interests. Eventually the conflict escalated into a full-scale war, deadlier than the Korean War and longer than any other in American history.

The uncertain goals of the war, the high casualties, and especially the fact that nearly 15 percent all U.S. infantrymen were black caused tremendous controversy in the African American community. In 1965 Malcolm X claimed that the U.S. government was "causing American soldiers to be murdered every day, for no reason at all." Two years later Martin Luther King, Jr., reminded the American public that "the Negro" had always managed to become a "100%

General Daniel "Chappie" James, the first black four-star general

citizen in warfare," but was always reduced to a "50% citizen on American soil."

One of the most famous black protesters of the war was heavyweight champion Muhammad Ali. A Black Muslim, Ali declared himself a **conscientious** objector on religious grounds. He was convicted of violating the Selective Service Act and stripped of his championship as well. In 1970 the Supreme Court cleared Ali of wrongdoing.

Still, most young black men were willing to answer the draft board's call when it came. Private First Class Milton Olive of Chicago was typical of blacks who risked, and sometimes lost, their lives during the war. Olive was killed by an exploding grenade on which he had fallen to save the lives of his comrades; the government acknowledged his heroism by awarding a posthumous Congressional Medal of Honor.

By mid-1969 nine other African Americans had joined Olive as recipients of the medal: Captain Riley L. Pitts; First Lieutenant Ruppert L. Sargent; Sergeants Rodney M. Davis, Matthew Leonard, and Donald R. Long; Specialists Five Lawrence Joel, Clarence E. Sasser, and Dwight H. Johnson; and Private First Class James Anderson, Jr.

According to *New York Times* reporter Thomas Johnson, officers in the Military

Brigadier General F. Davison (right center) discusses strategy with Captain Oliver E. Murray (left center) in South Vietnam, 1968

Assistance Command said that the 173rd Airborne Brigade, a crack outfit with a heavy black representation, was "the best performing unit in Vietnam." In such elite combat units, one out of every four combat troops was a black man.

The 1970s and 1980s

In 1972, a year before the final withdrawal of U.S. troops from Vietnam, the Defense Department issued "The Search for Military Justice." This report recognized that discrimination still existed in the military. In particular, it found that blacks and Hispanics were involved in more disciplinary incidents and were punished more severely.

At the time blacks represented about 13 percent of discharged servicemen but received 33 percent of the dishonorable discharges, 21 percent of bad conduct discharges, 16 percent of undesirable discharges, and 20 percent of general discharges. Less than honorable discharges can brand a person for life, threatening one's career and earning ability—and veterans' benefits.

Fortunately, high-ranking government and military officials are moving to eliminate such abuses. Today, in many ways, military life is less discriminatory than civilian life. And beginning in the 1980s, increasing numbers of women joined the military, working side by side with men in a variety of areas.

By the end of the decade, blacks represented 28 percent of the total enlisted Army force, while black women numbered nearly 45 percent of enlisted women. Yet recruiting blacks as officers was difficult in the 1980s due in part to competition with industry, law schools, and the professions, all of which pursued young black men and women with offers of higher salaries than those offered by the military.

Nonetheless, throughout this period one black career officer, especially, was demonstrating that the military was allowing African Americans to rise to the highest positions of leadership and prestige. That officer was Colin Powell, who in 1989 was named to the most powerful military position in the United States: chairman of the Joint Chiefs of Staff.

The Persian Gulf War

If Powell's name did not become a household word with this appointment, it certainly did with the advent of the Gulf War in 1991.

African Americans were deeply divided over American involvement in the Gulf War, with almost half of those polled at the time opposed to it. Several black leaders, including Representative Charles Rangel of New York, were concerned in particular about the high number of blacks fighting to liberate Kuwait from Iraq. Powell himself initially favored economic sanctions (embargoes) over military actions, until war became the stated policy of President George Bush. From then on, Powell earned credit for drafting and putting into action a brilliant campaign—which began with the largest single air attack in history—that minimized the loss of American lives.

About 104,000 of the 400,000 troops serving in the Persian Gulf were black. According to the Department of Defense, blacks

General Hazel Johnson

accounted for 30 percent of the Army, 21 percent of the Navy, 17 percent of the Marines, and 14 percent of the Air Force personnel stationed in the Gulf (in 1991 blacks comprised only 12.4 percent of the U.S. population). For Powell, the high participation of blacks, as shown by the Gulf War numbers, is a positive, rather than a negative: "To those who question the proportion of blacks in the armed services, my answer is simple. The military of the United States is the greatest equal opportunity employer around."

Although the debate over blacks in the military will likely continue, virtually everyone agrees that Powell has been and

Powell signs an autograph during the Persian Gulf War

continues to serve as an important role model for young African Americans:

[The] message I give to young people as I talk in high schools essentially says, "Do not let the fact that you're a minority or that you come from a different background or that you are trapped structurally somewhere serve as an anchor to keep you down. You've got to swim against it, you've got to climb against it."

◀ Chairman of the Joint Chiefs of Staff Colin Powell salutes after laying a wreath at the Vietnam Veterans Memorial, 1991

FURTHER READING

Aptheker, Herbert, ed., *A Documentary History of the Negro People in the United States,* New York: Carol Publishing Group, 1990.

Bennett, Lerone, *Before the Mayflower,* 6th ed., Chicago: Johnson Publishing Company, 1987.

Berry, Mary Frances, and John W. Blassingame, *Long Memory: The Black Experience in America,* New York and Oxford: Oxford University Press, 1982.

Billingsley, Andrew, *Climbing Jacob's Ladder: The Enduring Legacy of African-American Families,* New York: Simon & Schuster, 1992.

Bing, Léon, *Do or Die,* New York: HarperCollins Publishers, 1991.

Bogle, Donald, *Toms, Coons, Mulattoes, Mammies, and Bucks: An Interpretive History of Blacks in American Films,* New York: Continuum Publishing Company, 1989.

Clark, Joe, with Joe Picard, *Laying Down the Law: Joe Clark's Strategy for Saving Our Schools,* Washington, D.C.: Regnery Gateway, 1989.

Collins, Charles M., and David Cohen, eds., *The African Americans,* New York: Viking Studio Books, 1993.

Copage, Eric V., *Black Pearls: Daily Meditations, Affirmations, and Inspirations for African Americans,* New York: William Morrow, 1993.

Durham, Michael S., *Powerful Days: The Civil Rights Photography of Charles Moore,* New York: Stewart, Tabori & Chang, 1991.

Edwards, Audrey, and Craig K. Polite, *Children of the Dream: The Psychology of Black Success,* New York: Doubleday, 1992.

Franklin, John Hope, and Alfred A. Moss, Jr., *From Slavery to Freedom: A History of Negro Americans,* New York: McGraw Hill, 1988.

Haber, Louis, *Black Pioneers of Science and Invention,* San Diego: Harcourt Brace Jovanovich, 1987.

Hampton, Henry, and Steve Fayer, *Voices of Freedom: An Oral History of the Civil Rights Movement from the 1950s through the 1960s,* New York: Bantam, 1990.

Hardnett, Carolyn J., and Dawne A. Johnson, "Black Year in Review," *Emerge,* December/January 1994, pp. 55-60.

Harley, Sharon, et al., *The African American Experience: A History,* Englewood Cliffs, New Jersey: Simon & Schuster, 1992.

Haskins, James, *Black Music in America: A History through Its People,* New York: Crowell Junior Books, 1987.

Hughes, Langston, Milton Meltzer, and C. Eric Lincoln, *A Pictorial History of Blackamericans,* New York: Crown Publishers, 1983.

Johnson, John H., with Lerone Bennett, Jr., *Succeeding against the Odds,* New York: Warner Books, 1989.

Kimbro, Dennis, *Daily Motivations for African-American Success,* New York: Fawcett Columbine, 1993.

King, Anita, ed., *Quotations in Black,* Westport, Connecticut: Greenwood Press, 1981.

Low, W. Augustus, and Virgil A. Clift, *Encyclopedia of Black America,* New York: McGraw Hill, 1981.

Marsh, Carole S., *Black Trivia: The African-American Experience, A-to-Z!,* Decatur, Georgia: Gallopade Publishing Group, 1992.

Mullane, Deirdre, ed., *Crossing the Danger Water: Three Hundred Years of African-American Writing,* New York: Doubleday, 1993.

Pelz, Ruth, *Black Heroes of the Wild West,* Seattle: Open Hand Publishing, 1990.

Salley, Columbus, *The Black 100: A Ranking of the Most Influential African-Americans, Past and Present,* New York: Carol Publishing Group, 1993.

Shaw, Arnold, *Black Popular Music in America,* New York: Schirmer Books, 1986.

Thum, Marcella, *Hippocrene U.S.A. Guide to Black America: A Directory of Historic and Cultural Sites Relating to Black America,* New York: Hippocrene Books, 1991.

Westridge Young Writers Workshop, *Kids Explore America's African-American Heritage,* Santa Fe, New Mexico: John Muir Publications, 1992.

INDEX